Going local

Who should run Britain's police?

**Barry Loveday
and Anna Reid**

First published in January 2003 by Policy Exchange

Policy Exchange
Clutha House
10 Storey's Gate
London SW1P 3AY
Tel: 020 7340 2650
www.policyexchange.org.uk

ISBN 1 84275 070 4
Typeset by Politico's Design, design@politicos.co.uk
Printed in Britain by Heron, Dawson and Sawyer

Contents

Executive summary

What is the best way to run a police force in modern Britain? What systems of accountability produce greatest success in fighting crime and restoring public confidence in the police? How can we learn from the successes and failures of policing in other countries? These are the questions that this study seeks to answer.

Yes, Minister

The recent history of policing in Britain has been one of increasing central control and weakening links between police and local communities:

- A Conservative government initiated a series of police force amalgamations that cut their number by two-thirds, so that many communities are now served by anonymous composite forces covering several counties.
- Another Conservative Government reduced the size of police authorities and the role of local councillors within them;
- Now a Labour Government has expanded the role of the Home Office in setting detailed targets, prescribing policing strategies, inspecting performance and requiring the implementation of detailed action plans.

Interviews with senior police officers, local councillors and MPs around the country provide striking evidence of the effects of centralisation:

- Police authorities are invisible and irrelevant. Nobody knows who sits on them or what they do – not even local MPs. They do not control the promotion of senior officers, the funding of police budgets or the measurement of police performance.
- Smaller forces with a strong commitment to visible policing are among the most successful at cutting crime and providing public reassurance. Analysis of the Government's own statistics provide no evidence that larger amalgamated forces are generally more effective or offer better value for money.
- Central intervention does not deliver. The recent, media-driven Safer Streets Initiative failed to cut street robbery in four out of the ten targeted forces. Where robbery did fall, it did so at the unreasonable cost of £14,500 per crime prevented. Now the government is requiring all police forces to adopt the specialist-led Kent Policing Model, although it has failed to win public confidence in the county where it was originally developed.

At the pleasure of the Mayor

In the United States, policing is directed, managed and financed locally. For most mayors and county boards, appointing the police chief and setting the policing budget are the most important powers they possess. Apart from dealing with a few federal crimes, the Federal Government's main role is to investigate and prosecute instances of corruption in local police forces and city halls. Although there have been several such cases in recent years, in general the US model of policing has chalked up some remarkable achievements.

- The Compstat management tool developed in New York gives senior officers week-by-week, precinct-by-precinct information on crime, transforming their ability to manage staff, shift resources to where the problems are, and respond rapidly to public concerns.

- The Broken Windows theory of policing has highlighted the importance of tackling graffiti and other threats to the quality of life in public spaces, so that law-abiding local people can reclaim the streets from criminals.

- Crime has fallen dramatically in communities ranging from tiny Arlington County, Virginia (where crime dropped 39% during the 1990s) to New York City (where crime dropped 61% from 1992 to 2001).

L'Etat c'est moi

In France, most policing is the responsibility of two centrally-run national forces. Public concern over a lack of visible policing prompted locally-elected mayors to set up their own municipal police forces. Central government has responded by reasserting central control over the municipal forces, and by encouraging the national forces to adopt a neighbourhood policing strategy. This has not worked: violent crime and fear of crime continue to rise, contributing to the success of the far-right in the spring 2002 presidential elections.

"Love thy neighbour" – policing in the Netherlands

Policing in the Netherlands is provided by regional forces whose chiefs report to centrally-appointed local officials. The system leads to confusion over policing priorities, and has allowed forces to become divorced from local people's concerns and prisoner to the politically correct preconceptions of a professional elite. An extreme version of community policing, recasting policemen as social workers, has failed to address rising violent crime and fear of crime. Public frustration with crime levels and the lack of police response contributed to the success of the anti-

immigration party List Pym Fortuyn in recent local and national elections.

Servants of the People

We conclude that British policing should be restructured as follows:

- Police should be made directly accountable to mayors and council leaders.

- Mayors and council leaders should be subject to overview and scrutiny by a policing committee and seek approval by elected assemblies and councils for the police budget and strategy.

- Chief Constables should be put on short term contracts, and hired and fired by mayors and council leaders.

- The convention of constabulary independence should be limited and defined in statute.

- Police forces should be locally financed.

- HMIC should focus on audit work especially corruption checks.

- A National Crime Agency should be established and take over the national policing functions of the Met as well as responsibility for investigating corruption in local government and police forces.

- A National Police Holding Body should be set up to handle the transition for residual police assets such as police colleges and forensic laboratories.

Introduction

Aims

The aim of this study is to examine ways in which the police forces of England and Wales might be made more effective in reducing crime and more accountable to the communities they serve. It does so by examining the strengths and weaknesses of the existing British systems of police service management and political accountability, and comparing them with those of the police services of the United States, the Netherlands and France.

Background

The study was undertaken from April to November 2002, against a background of general malaise within British policing and local government.

Recent years have seen recorded crime rise and detection rates fall, whilst fear of crime stays persistently high. Public dissatisfaction with policing has crystallised around demands for more 'bobbies on the beat' and for more emphasis on tackling minor crime and anti-social behaviour. Police forces have become increasingly resentful of tighter central government control, and central government increasingly impatient with forces' low detection rates and resistance to modern management techniques and working practices.

At the same time, local government has lost power and public respect. Typically, three-quarters of a local authority's funding comes from central rather than local taxation, and much of that money is 'ring-fenced', leaving authorities with no discretion over spending. Fewer people are willing to serve as councillors, and there are doubts as to the calibre of many of those who do serve. Turnouts in local election rarely top 50%, and those for the most recent round of mayoral referenda were even lower, at under 30%.

The study tests the hypothesis that giving local communities more power, via elected representatives, over their police forces would both improve policing and revive local government. An ICM poll commissioned by Policy Exchange in April 2002 suggested that half of all voters would be more likely to participate in local

Table 1: Crime and policing statistics (1997-2002)					
	1997/98	1998/99	1999/00	2000/01	2001/02
Officer Numbers (FTE)(England & Wales)	126,814	126,096	124,170	125,682	129,603
Spend on Crime (£)(England & Wales)	7.02bn	7.23bn	7.44bn	7.72bn	8.5bn
Total Recorded Crime	4,545,337	5,109,089	5,301,187	5,170,843	5,527,082
Detection Rate (%)	28	29	25	24	23
Percentage of the public perceiving increased crime	n/a	59	67	56	64

Sources: Home Office; BCS 2002

elections if they were able to vote directly for 'the people who run your local public services - such as the local Chief Constable or chief executive of the local NHS Trust.' 80% of those polled said they wanted more input into public service priority-setting, and 58% thought standards would improve under an elective system, as compared with just 7% who feared they would get worse (see Appendix A).

How can local communities be given a greater say in how they are policed? How can police forces be made more responsive to public demands, whilst remaining impartial in their enforcement of the law? How can central government's responsibilities be married with local freedoms to meet local sensitivities and needs? It is a mark of the extent to which these and related questions resonate within the police service that in the course of research for this report many senior officers showed themselves well aware of a need for more local accountability, and open-minded about potential mechanisms for achieving it.

Methodology

The study examines five representative UK police forces, covering a range of areas, from the heavily urban (the Metropolitan Police), to the county-based mixed urban and rural (Kent, Nottinghamshire and Hampshire) and heavily rural (Dyfed Powys). Case studies of two specific initiatives - the government's Safer Streets campaign and Kent Constabulary's Kent Policing Model - illustrate the practical effects of tight central control combined with a lack of accountability to local communities.

The study also includes a performance league table of all English and Welsh police forces, drawn up using data from Her Majesty's Inspectorate of Constabulary, the Crown Prosecution Service and the British Crime Survey (BCS). Modelled on the Home Office's proposed 'spidergram' analysis (currently not due for launch until April 2004), the analysis highlights enormous variations in quality between forces, demonstrates that small forces are at least as effective as large ones, and suggests that the forces covering the largest conurbations - London, Leeds, Manchester and the West Midlands - are relatively underfunded. The league table also demonstrates some of the weaknesses of management by performance indicator, it being extremely difficult to select indicators that are useful and robust, to weight them appropriately, and to ensure that data are consistent across forces. (For a summary of the league table research, see Appendix B.)

Three policing systems abroad are examined: those of the United States, where financing is heavily local and accountability is to a variety of locally-elected representatives, of the Netherlands, where force amalgamations are in progress and accountability is to centrally-appointed local officials, and of France, where the development of municipal forces has produced problems of overlap with the gendarmerie and police nationale, as well as increased accountability to city halls. A case study of Compstat (Computer Statistics),

an internal management tool first developed by the New York Police Department and now adopted by forces elsewhere, demonstrates an alternative to Home Office-style centralised management by centrally-collected performance indicator.

1. Recent developments in UK policing

The Trend Towards Centralisation

The study was undertaken during the passage into law of the 2002 Police Reform Act. Ostensibly concerned to drive up police performance, it gives the Home Secretary significantly greater powers of intervention in force management, and is the latest in a long line of centralizing measures introduced, despite considerable resistance from police and parliament, by both Labour and Conservative governments:

The 1964 Police Act

The 1964 Act introduced a 'tripartite' relationship between Chief Constable, Home Secretary and Police Authority, under which the Home Secretary and police authorities jointly shared responsibility for police performance. The relationship was not, however, one of equals, since the Home Secretary remained in control of police force finances, and got new powers to veto Watch Committees' (the forerunners to police authorities) decisions to hire or fire Chief Constables. Chief Constables were simultaneously given considerable autonomy under the convention (already long established in case law) of constabulary independence. Section 5(1) of the Act stipulated: '*the police force maintained for a police area shall be under the direction and control of the chief constable.*' Police authorities had only a monitoring role, and the ability to call upon Chief Constables for reports.

The Act came under strain in the early 1980s, when police authorities in large Labour-controlled cities - London, Manchester, Liverpool and Birmingham - began to exercise their powers under the Act more aggressively, regularly demanding that Chief Constables submit reports on a wide variety of policing matters. This brief period of enhanced local accountability ended in 1985, when Margaret Thatcher's government abolished the Greater London Council and metropolitan county councils.

Force amalgamations, 1968-1974

Successive rounds of force amalgamation reduced the total number of forces in England and Wales from 126 in 1968 to 43 in 1974. The restructuring began under Harold Wilson's Labour government, and was completed by a Conservative one under Edward Heath. Objections (never very strong) from the police were overridden on the grounds that amalgamations would produce cost savings and better policing.

The 1993 Sheehy Inquiry into Police Rewards and Responsibilities

In a detailed report, the Sheehy Inquiry made a large number of recommendations on modernizing police pay, conditions and management structures. It was, however, poorly presented by Home Secretary Kenneth Clarke and implacably resisted by the police, resulting therefore in only minor changes that were themselves subsequently watered down. Though the report recommended fixed-term contracts and performance-related pay for all officers, these were in fact only applied to officers of ACPO rank (i.e. Assistant Chief Constable and above). The ranks of Deputy Chief Constable and Chief Inspector, abolished by Sheehy, have since made a return.

The 1994 Police and Magistrates Courts Act, and the 1996 Police Act

The 1994 and '96 Acts reduced the size of police authorities (usually from 35 members to 17), and transferred direct management functions and control over budgets from them to Chief Constables (acting within limits set by the Home Office.) Previously, two-thirds of authority members had been elected, the remaining third consisting of magistrates. Since the Acts, a simple majority are chosen from amongst elected councillors, and the remainder drawn from the magistracy or appointed as 'independents' with Home Office approval. Authority functions dwindled to choosing Chief Constables from shortlists drawn up by the Home Office, agreeing policing plans drawn up by Chief Constables, monitoring police performance, and sustaining consultation mechanisms with the public.

In early, more centralizing, drafts, the Acts gave the Home Secretary power to select police authority chairmen, and cut the number of police forces in England and Wales by half, the rationale being that the creation of Basic Command Units (BCUs) in 1992 had done away with the need for many force headquarters. These measures were only dropped following rejection by the House of Lords.

The 1998 Crime and Disorder Act

The 1998 Crime and Disorder Act created 'Crime and Disorder Reduction Partnerships' (CDRPs) between police forces and local authorities. Under these, local authorities carry out regular 'crime audits' of their area, drawing on opinion polls, focus groups, and feedback from local health, education, social security, housing and other departments. On the basis of these, local authorities and police jointly draw up Crime Reduction Strategies, which they have joint statutory responsibility to see effectively implemented.

Though CDRPs seem generally to have been a success, with both local authorities and police regarding them as useful, they have not made the public feel they have an input into local policing. A survey of Londoners in 2001 found that only 9% of respondents had heard of them, and they did not crop up at all in researchers' focus groups [Fitzgerald *et al* 2002].

The 2002 Police Reform Act

Coming into force in October 2002, the Act hands significant new powers to the Home Secretary, via an empowered Her Majesty's Inspectorate of Constabulary (HMIC) and a new Police Standards Unit . The Home Secretary is enabled to draw up annual national policing plans and new codes of practice, and to require police authorities to produce 'Action Plans' for failing forces. Whereas previously, he could only require Chief Constables to retire in the interests of 'efficiency and effectiveness', he can now require them to resign, meaning that they lose pension rights. The Act also requires forces to adopt the National Intelligence Model of policing, currently seen as representing best practice in the use of criminal intelligence and information technology.

In its original draft, the 2002 Act would have allowed the Home Secretary directly to require failing Chief Constables to produce plans for remedial action. Following opposition in the House of Lords, this was watered down so that he can now only do so via the police authority, and in respect of matters where the force has been specifically criticised by HMIC.

HMIC and the Police Standards Unit

It is likely that the 2002 Act's most significant innovation will come to be seen as the creation of the Police Standards Unit (PSU), based within and reporting directly to the Home Office. Operational since July 2001, its role, as laid out in the White Paper *Policing a New Century: a Blueprint for Reform* [Home Office, 2001] which presaged the Act, is to identify good practice 'in the prevention, detection and apprehension of crime', and how best to spread it [CM 2001:128]. When it identifies a force as in need of 'remedial actions', it can provide short-term funds for these to be undertaken. By late

September 2002 the Unit had already intervened in 23 forces at risk of missing targets for burglaries and vehicle crime [*Police Review* 27/19/02], and with another ten under the government's £67m Safer Streets campaign against street robbery.

The Act also makes it clear that HMIC will continue to exercise a significant role in monitoring police force performance. It is given power to inspect police authorities' Best Value reviews and individual BCUs, and expected to work closely with the PSU. The White Paper looked forward to it 'continuing to develop a more radical and challenging approach to inspecting the police service':

> 'Increasingly [HMIC's] focus is on the most critical performance issues of crime reduction, delivery of targets, leadership and public reassurance. The Government is committed to refocusing, identifying and challenging the worst performers and recognizing and celebrating the best' [CM5326 2001:130].

In fulfilling their new responsibilities, both HMIC and the PSU are expected heavily to rely on a reduced number of centrally determined performance indicators (PIs), seen as the cornerstone of all the Act's reforms [CM 5326 2001:132].

The National Policing Plan

Data from HMIC and the PSU will inform an annual National Policing Plan, drawn up by the Home Secretary and providing 'a clear sense of where the Government believes the police service should be going' [CM 5326:132]. Prepared by November 30th each year, the Plan will identify the government's three-year strategic priorities for policing, how they are to be delivered and the indicators by which performance will be measured. It will provide the basis for issuing ministerial objectives and performance targets, and include 'such other information, plans and advice as the Secretary of State considers relevant' [Police Reform Explanatory Notes 2002:7].

The first such National Policing Plan, published on November 20th 2002, lays down 51 'actions that chief officers and police authorities should take account of in local policing plans', 19 of which have specific targets attached.

The Act also empowers the Home Secretary to make national regulations laying down specific 'procedures or practices' whereby chief officers are to ' police the force area or in relation to the way they run their force'. This must be done, however, in consultation with the Association of Police Authorities (APA), Association of Chief Police Officers (ACPO), HMIC and CPTDA.

The National Intelligence Model

The White Paper emphasizes that an integral feature of future policing will be the National Intelligence Model (NIM). Seen as being at the forefront of current policing theory and practice, the NIM sets out what is intended to be a focused approach to the gathering and use of criminal intelligence, and promotes cooperation between forces [CM5326 2001:45]. The National Criminal

Intelligence Service has identified suitable computer systems to support its use, following specifications developed by ACPO. All forces are now required to adopt the core of NIM, although 'some local discretion' may be allowed [CM 2001:45]. Implementation will be overseen by HMIC and the PSU. While it is probably too early to make any considered judgement concerning NIM, it can be expected to be manpower intensive and to reduce visible uniformed presence on the streets.

The Accountability Gap

Despite a forty-year centralizing trend in British policing, its benefits are far from proven. On the public's part, fear of crime and lack of faith in the police have risen. Growing numbers of victims fail to report crimes, in the belief that the police are either unwilling or unable to do anything about them: 35% of violent attacks by strangers, 38% of burglaries, 42% of thefts from vehicles and 58% of muggings went unreported in 2001 [CM 5326:23].

A matter of equal concern, identified by British Crime Surveys and elsewhere, is the perception that forces are withdrawing from their communities. Particularly unpopular is the closure of local police stations and their replacement by 'mobile' stations and distant call-centres. Similarly, the public continue to regard a visible uniformed police presence on the streets as a key part of policing, and as basic evidence of the maintenance of law and order. Moves towards larger units and more specialization - in other words towards fewer local stations and fewer 'bobbies on the beat' - have clearly, therefore, been counterproductive in terms of the basic police function of public reassurance [Loveday 1998].

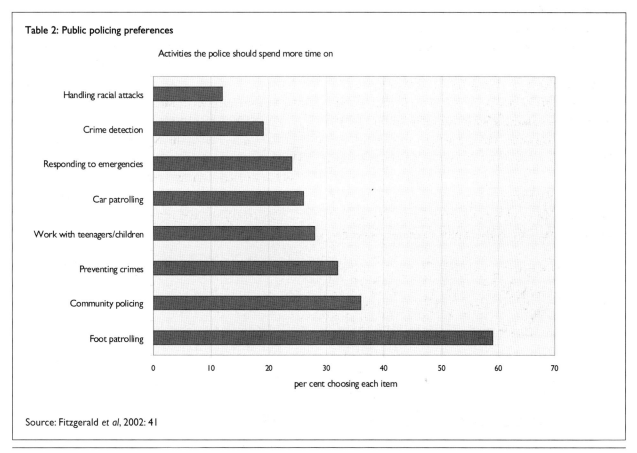

Table 2: Public policing preferences

Activities the police should spend more time on

per cent choosing each item

Source: Fitzgerald *et al*, 2002: 41

Police Authorities

The Conservative police reforms of the mid-1990s left police authorities neither powerful nor very democratic. Member numbers were typically reduced from 35 to 17, of whom nine are elected, drawn from local councillors, three are magistrates and five independents, chosen by the rest of the membership in conjunction with the Home Secretary. The nine councillor-members are drawn from political parties in proportion to their share of the local vote, meaning that many local authority districts are left unrepresented. Larger city authorities, with up to 25 members, experience the same problem.

> " some process of election should be seriously considered "

Early drafts of the incoming Labour government's Crime and Disorder legislation of 1997-8 excluded police authorities from new Crime and Disorder Reduction Partnerships between local authorities and police forces. Although authorities were finally included in the CDRPs by the Police Reform Act 2002, in practice it is district and borough councils that have used them most effectively. This was acknowledged during the House of Lords' debate on the 2002 Act. Defending the proposal that Chief Constables alone be allowed whether to deploy Community Support Officers, a government minister stated:

'I accept that the police authority members have a role as a voice on behalf of the general public. That is their function. But no one is going to kid me or anyone else that they actually represent anyone. Let us not beat about the bush. The fact is that if one person in three knows the name of his member of Parliament, I doubt whether more than one person in a thousand knows the name of any member of the police authority in his area'. [Lord Rooker, Hansard Col 828].

The problem of the role and membership of the police authorities was raised again in the House of Commons:

Mr Hughes [Lib Dem]: 'Does not my Hon. Friend agree that we need to consider whether police authorities are adequately responsive to their communities? Perhaps rather than expecting the Government to solve every problem across every department we should look again at whether police authorities require alteration to their structure. Already greater influence is exerted at borough and local command unit level, which may be because people feel that the police authority structure is too remote for local community needs, which differ even within one police force area.'

Mr Jones [Labour]: ' I agree with the Hon. Member for Southwark North and Bermondsey. We should discuss reform of local police authorities, but the Bill does not cover that. The Liberal Democrats try to present a utopian vision of local police authorities that are somehow in touch with what happens locally or are representative. I cannot accept that.... I remind members that a Conservative government interfered directly in police authorities in 1994 when they reduced the number of county councillors who served on them. They also provided that the Home Secretary has a direct influence on appointments to police authorities'.

Mr Hogg [Conservative]: 'The Hon. Member for Lewes made a point of some substance in saying that the police authority's accountability to the local community should be reinforced. I think this House should seriously debate how the police authority can be made more accountable to the local community... **I would have thought that some** process of election should be seriously considered. Whether one would confine it to the chairmanship or membership of the police authority is a matter for debate.'

Mr Letwin [Conservative]: 'There was a time when the Labour party believed that there was a real argument for localism - at least in the context of policing. There was also a time when the Conservative party believed that there was much to be gained ... by trying to bring about more effectiveness from the centre. Labour have become more and more enchanted by the idea of taking action from the centre ... [while] we have become increasingly sceptical of the value of centralised intervention and increasingly attentive to the long term sustainable advantages of localism. That is a most interesting shift in the character of politics.'[Hansard Parliamentary Debates, Cols 933-941].

Parliament's views were borne out in interview with a representative of the Association of Police Authorities. In her view, authorities' 'independents' are often much more effective than their councillor-members, providing a range of backgrounds and experience that councillors lack. The independents on her own, big-city authority included Hindu and Moslem clerics, a drug counsellor, and a former management consultant. They had, she said, 'been brilliant', providing something approaching a 'board of directors, with a range of skills.' Her Labour councillor-members, in contrast, tended to be ex-trade unionists, with experience that 'isn't always very relevant to policing', and her Conservative ones to be 65 years old or more, and unfamiliar with urban and youth issues. She also felt that police authorities, as currently constituted, fail to make use of the powers they have:

'I don't feel that I need any extra powers, because I use the ones I've got to the full. But I've got

colleagues up and down the country who don't. Police chiefs get up on their high horse, and you have to be a very confident person to challenge them [Interview, Local Government House, 2002].'

It would be easier to challenge Chief Constables, she thought, if more police funding came out of local taxation. Though police authorities already have a say in deciding how much of the central grant to local government is passed on to police forces, 'it would give councillors more clout if it was their own, locally-raised money that they were dispersing rather than Whitehall funds.'

Despite this consensus on police authorities' failings, the 2002 Act left their membership and powers largely unchanged. As was argued by the Minister for Police, John Denham, it was 'not the time to change the composition of police authorities.' [Hansard Col 943 10/7/02].

Constabulary Independence

The accountability problem is complicated by the ancient and somewhat mysterious convention of constabulary independence [Marshall, Lustgarten, Reiner 2001]. Developed in case law from 1930 [*Fisher vs. Oldham Corporation*[1]], the convention was originally designed to protect the police from political interference in upholding the law, and gives Chief Constables control over all 'operational' as opposed to strategic policing matters. As observed earlier, it was first enshrined in statute in the 1964 Police Act, which states that '*The police force shall be under the direction and control of the chief constable* [Section 5(1)].'

In practice, constabulary independence has simultaneously undermined police authorities' status, and been undermined itself by extensions to the Home Secretary's powers.

Much to blame is the lack of any definition of what constitute 'operational' as opposed to 'non-operational' policing matters. In the landmark case of *R. vs. Commissioner of the Metropolis ex parte Blackburn* in

1968[2], the Commissioner argued that he could not be required to devote more resources to policing gambling clubs, despite the fact that they had become centres of prostitution. He was backed by the Court of Appeal. Twenty years later, a second case, *R vs. Secretary of State for the Home Department ex parte Northumbria Police Authority*[3], pitted police authorities against Chief Constables and central government, the issue at stake being whether or not Northumbria police should be issued with CS gas and plastic bullets. Again, the Court of Appeal backed the Chief Constable, ruling that he could have gas and bullets if HMIC considered them necessary. Most recently, in the 1999 case of *R vs. Chief Constable of Sussex ex parte International Traders Ferry Limited*[4], the courts upheld the Chief Constable of Sussex's right not to remove demonstrators who were preventing the export of live veal calves from the port of Shoreham, despite the claimant's argument that this put the UK in breach of EU free trade rules [Reiner 2000: 190-6].

> ❝ there is interference by stealth in the operational objectives of all police forces ❞

The definitional problem was highlighted in parliamentary debate on the Police Reform Act 2002. An opposition spokesman noted, in relation to the Home Secretary's proposed new power to issue action plans for failed forces, that the fundamental principle being dealt with was that of the operational independence of chief constables. It was hard, however, to formulate precise definitions for 'operational' and 'non-operational', because 'strategy melds into operation in a way that is difficult for legislation to disentangle in advance' [Hansard Col 916]. In reply, the Labour Member for Nottingham North (Nottinghamshire being one the ten

'failing forces' targeted by the government's Safer Streets campaign), observed that:

> 'Unless we put into the Police Reform Bill a definition of at least part of what we all agree is operational, the very thing that he fears will happen. Home Secretaries of all political colours will not only set targets but ensure that money is allocated to meeting them, so it becomes almost inevitable that Chief Constables and local police officers will have to pursue those targets. In that way, there is interference almost by stealth in the operational objectives of all police forces. If we were now to debate honestly what is operational and what is not, the difference would be clearer not only to us but to officers on the ground and senior officers in local constabularies.' [Hansard Col 916/917].

During the bill's second reading, in contrast, the same MP stressed Chief Constables' own misuse of the convention of constabulary independence against elected representatives:

> 'The concept of an operational requirement has been respected by politicians for many years, but is it respected by senior police officers? The boundary between what is and is not operational is increasingly being pushed back [by them].' [Hansard Col 915]

The Independent Commission on Policing in Northern Ireland, led by Chris Patten, took a similar line:

> 'One of the most difficult issues we have considered is the question of 'operational independence'. Some respondents urged us to define operational independence or at least define the powers and responsibilities of the police...The Police Authority told us that under the present arrangements if a

Chief Constable decided that a matter was operational, and therefore within the scope of police independence, there was nothing that they could do to pursue it... The term 'operational independence' is neither to be found in nor is defined in any legislation. It is an extrapolation from the phrase 'direction and control' included in statutory descriptions of the functions of Chief Constables. But however it may be defined it is not acceptable that the scrutiny of the police should be impeded by the assertion, valid or otherwise, that the current legislation empowering such scrutiny is limited to such matters outside the scope of operational independence... Long consideration has led us to the view that the term 'operational independence' is itself a large part of the problem. In a democratic society all public officials must be fully accountable to the institutions of that society for the due performance of their functions, and a chief of police cannot be an exception. No public official including a chief of police can be said to be 'independent'. Indeed given the extraordinary powers conferred on the police it is essential that their exercise is subject to the closest and most effective scrutiny possible' [Report of the Independent Commission on Northen Ireland 1999:6.19-6.20].

The Patten Report concluded with a recommendation that the term 'operational responsibility' be substituted for that of 'operational independence', within the proposed Police Act for Northern Ireland, making it clear that an operational matter could not be exempt from subsequent review 'by anyone' [Report 1999:6.21]. The change was not adopted.

Performance Targets

Unfettered by a firm definition of Chief Constables' 'operational' responsibilities, central government has been able to make increasing use of policing performance targets, further throwing into doubt the principle of constabulary independence. Targets were first introduced by a Conservative government, in the Police and Magistrate Courts Acts of 1994 and 1996, and have since been considerably extended. As recently noted by former Chief Constable of Bedfordshire, Michael O'Byrne:

'Section 38 of the [1996 Police] Act gives the Home Secretary the power to establish...performance targets. Assurances were given at the time that it would not be used to set 'hard' targets for individual forces. However, the language of the section allows this, and...it is clear from the performance regime under which the service now labours that these hard targets have now been set, whether or not the Home Secretary wishes to hold the chief constable or police authority to account under this particular section.' [O'Byrne 2001:119]

The push towards wider use of performance targets has largely come from HMIC, whose annual force inspection reports have long stressed the need for forces to adopt a 'performance culture.'

The limitations and perverse effects of target-setting in policing, as in other public services, are now well-established [Fitzgerald *et al* 2002; Neyroud and Beckley 2001]. As argued by a former Conservative Home Office minister during the debate on the 2002 Police Reform Act, they tend to distort policing priorities, tempting officers into using their time in unproductive ways or into directly fiddling performance figures:

'Nowadays everything is about setting targets...In the case of policing that is difficult as it is in the case of the NHS. People end up trying to chase the target and ensuring that they achieve it. That becomes the pre-eminent factor whereas the people being served are secondary. I remember when one of the targets was the number of cases resolved. The police have been known to go to people in prison to ask if they did this or that. If they said yes, the number of cases resolved rose and the target was achieved. That was not the right way to proceed. I am concerned that the police will find themselves fettered by the targets and all their efforts will go to achieving them as opposed to achieving better policing' [Earl Ferrers, Hansard Col 730].

The point is backed up by O'Byrne:

'Experience in policing and of any other organiza-tion...shows that when robust performance management comes in the door, ethics tend to go out through the window...Those whose perform-ance is being measured will move through a range of tactics to avoid, subvert or superficially satisfy the measurement regime. [O'Byrne 2001:94].'

The first response of an organization to such perform-ance regimes, O'Byrne goes on, is simply to question the validity of the basic data being collected, particularly if it is unfavourable. Thereafter working practices remain unchanged but ways of describing and reporting them adapt to satisfy the regime. Where employees do respond they focus on those elements of the regime which are most easily satisfied, 'at the expense of concentrating on what is important but is either difficult to achieve and /or difficult to measure. [O'Byrne 2001:94].'

> " when performance management comes in the door, ethics tend to go out the window "

Numerous studies attest to the way in which manage-ment by performance target encourages 'accountancy dodges.' According to a 2001 study of the Metropolitan Police [Fitzgerald et al 2002], targets for burglary reduc-tion prompt officers to record thefts from garden sheds and outhouses as thefts rather than burglaries, and attempted burglaries where premises are entered but nothing taken as 'criminal damage.' Similarly, it was recently revealed that Scotland's second-largest force, Lothian and Borders, had dramatically improved its detection rate by recording stabbings and other serious attacks as 'minor assaults' [The Times 22.11.02.]. An HMIC Thematic Review on Police Integrity of 1999 found that rank-and-file officers came under pressure from senior ones to target 'volume' crime at the expense of more serious incidents:

'There was evidence in one force that a divisional commander refused to allow his detectives to put more than minimal resources into a serious sexual crime investigation, preferring instead to concentrate their efforts on less serious crime such as car theft. This occurred because whether they solved a rape or the theft of a car radio, the division would only be credited with one detection [HMIC 1999:4.6].'

The sheer amount of time taken up by information recording is widely resented: 70% of officers, a survey found, agree with the statement 'I have to deal with too much bureaucracy to get my job done' [Fitzgerald et al 2002]. Analysis of the diaries of 378 beat officers in seven different BCUs round the country discovered that dealing with paper-work unconnected with prosecution files takes an average 12% of officers' total shift time. Some of this time is wasted by the inadequacy of police information technology systems, but the researchers 'also wondered whether officers are simply being asked to report too much.' In one BCU, 105 different reporting forms were found to be in regular use, leading an officer to complain that 'we're a reporting organ-ization, no longer a proactive force' [PA Consulting 2001].

Centrally-set performance targets also stifle local innovation and accountability, as highlighted by a recent report from the left-leaning think-tank the Institute of Public Policy Research:

'There is undoubtedly a need to improve the performance of all the criminal justice agencies. Government has a role in setting some national standards. But the centrally driven outcomes agenda, with its proliferation of targets and key performance indicators against which the agencies are measured, named and shamed, has limited their autonomy to determine their own priorities or to be innovative in developing new approaches. Moreover, it significantly limits the extent to which the public can influence local priorities. Consultation can become an opportunity only to explain why the local agency is constrained by national requirements from responding to local demands [IPPR Criminal Justice Forum, 2002:ix].'

The report recommends that the government should cut the number of centrally-set targets and indicators, allowing for greater local innovation and autonomy, and abandon the use of performance data to 'name and shame' failing agencies, since this only undermines public confidence in them [IPPR 2002:46].

Drawing up its own league table of police forces, based on data drawn from HMIC, the CPS and BCS, Policy Exchange discovered at first hand the many difficulties attendant on trying quantitatively to compare performance across forces (see Appendix B). Many performance indicators were regarded as unreliable and pointless by police officers interviewed for the research, and decisions about which of the remainder to include in the league table calculations, and how to weight them, involved subjective judgments as to the primary purpose of policing. It was also difficult to ensure that measurement of data was consistent across forces, notably in the area of crime recording, since some forces had adopted new reporting standards earlier than others. Less easily quantifiable policing functions - such as community-building, race relations improvement etc - were left out of the calculations altogether, and others, such as the percentage of cases passed to the CPS taken to court, partly depended on the performance of agencies other than the police.

Despite these criticisms from across the political spectrum, the government remains committed to the use of performance indicators in centrally managing the police. Allowing forces to fail in the name of local autonomy, debate on the 2002 Act made clear, is not an option:

'Where under-performance has been identified in a geographical area such as a Basic Command Unit, or in one particular area of policing - for example the reduction of burglary - the Home Secretary should be able to stop the rot before it spreads. He should be able to require early and effective remedial action to be taken rather than to have to sit back powerless while the performance of the force as a whole begins to suffer.' [Lord Bassam, Hansard Col 738].

The Act itself states that 'reliable comparative data on the efficiency and effectiveness of forces will be a crucial tool for the PSU, HMIC, police authorities and forces themselves in identifying and disseminating best practice, and raising the performance of all to the standards of the best [CM 5326 2001:7 18/19].'

Notes

1   [1930] 2 K.B. 364
2   [1968] 1 All E.R. 763
3   [1988] 2 W.L.R. 590
4   [1999] 1 All E.R. 129

2. UK reforms: making things better or worse?

Interviews with Police Officers and Local Politicians

Introduction

To canvass UK police officers' and local government members' views on accountability issues, we conducted interviews in five varied police force areas: London, Dyfed Powys, Kent, Hampshire and Nottinghamshire. London, of course, is the most densely-populated city in Britain, and has the largest police force, with 26,000 police officers and 11,412 civilian staff. Dyfed is the most sparsely-populated region of the country, and its force employs only 1,052 officers and 367 civilian personnel, making it roughly the same size as one of London's 32 borough-based BCUs. Kent, Hampshire and Nottinghamshire are traditional county forces, each encompassing a mix of small cities, towns and rural areas, as well as, in Kent's case, stretches of London's suburbia.

We also carried out case studies of two recent policing initiatives, one - the Safer Streets campaign of April-September 2002 - initiated by central government, the other - the Kent Policing Model - developed by a local force.

Performance indicators

The Home Office's use of performance indicators and targets came, perhaps not surprisingly, under attack from nearly all the officers interviewed. Common complaints were that they encompassed useless or already well-known information, that they skewed policing priorities, that collecting them took too much time, and that they failed to take into account local conditions, or causes of crime outside the police's control.

Typical was a comment from the current Chief Constable of Dyfed Powys. The vast bulk of performance indicators, in his opinion, are pointless, and in general accumulating numerical outputs is 'no good and little use'. In Nottinghamshire, indicators were criticised as simplistic, and as missing a wider picture. The Chief Constable of Hampshire complained that the Home Office's indicators excluded important measures such as

Table 3: Selected UK police forces					
	Dyfed Powys	Hampshire	Kent	Met	Notts
Population	482,800	1,796,700	1,598,033	7,368,694	1,032,200
Population Density (persons per hectare)	0.44	4.32	4.28	43.35	4.67
Police Officers (FTE)	1,131	3,480	3,355	26,223	2,330
Net Budget 2001/02	£65.3m	£27.8m	£206.6m	£2,200m	£148.3m
Recorded Crimes 2001/02	24,003	135,961	120,155	1,057,360	159,240

Source: Home Office; forces

numbers of road deaths and incidents of violence against children. Like others, he also thought that they set up perverse incentives, so that 'only what got measured got done.' In a fourth officer's words, they were 'unimaginative, about preserving the status quo', and 'monstrously bureaucratic, loaded with all the PC baggage you'd expect.'

A Commander at the Metropolitan Police had to collect data for eleven performance indicators covering serious crimes, and another 29 covering less serious crimes and organizational matters. In general, he was very supportive of the new performance culture within the police, and found statistical data vital in managing his own seven borough-level BCUs. The first things he looked at each day were crime trends and spending by area; other useful measures were convictions per officer and percentage of officers on front-line duties. Not all performance indicators, however, were as valuable. Though they were continually being refined and improved, many still took more time to collect than they were worth, and told him little that he did not know already: 'My daughter has this song. The bear climbs the mountain to see what he can see. And when he gets to the top, guess what he sees - another mountain! It's a very profound song.'

Administrative glitches in data collection could also lead to problems. Reading a management report, he was alarmed to discover that it took one of his BCUs an average sixty days to arrest suspects identified by crime-scene DNA analysis. 'The answer came back - Oh, we make the arrest within 24 hours, but we take two months to update the computer.'

The same officer also pointed out that criticism of performance indicators can be self-serving:

'We used to always complain about the performance indicators because the Met tended to come out badly. But now the Met's doing better, so suddenly the PIs are fair [Interview, Territorial Policing HQ, 2002].'

This was borne out by reactions to Policy Exchange's (admittedly simplified and provisional) league table of police forces, drawn up using HMIC, CPS and BCS data from April 2000-April 2002. Whereas forces at the top of the table tended to assume that it did indeed represent reality, ones at the bottom argued that the data used were flawed, or the comparisons made unfair.

A Hampshire Performance Review manager stressed the difficulty of enforcing consistent crime recording standards, without which it is hard to compare performance across forces:

'Many police processes are necessarily fuzzy at the edges. People in one part of the country may feel a minor theft or assault is a crime, and people in another part may not. One officer may feel an incident is a crime and another may not. Is throwing an egg against a door criminal damage? What exactly counts as harassment? PIs and performance management do influence decision-making in these fuzzy areas...An example is vehicle crime - when a victim reports that the lock or window of her car has been damaged, but nothing has been stolen. Was this an attempted theft of the vehicle, an attempted theft from the vehicle, criminal damage to the vehicle or vehicle interference? Under the current Home Office rules, only the first two count as vehicle crime [Hampshire Police HQ, Winchester, 2002].'

The Police Standards Unit and the threat of increased centralisation

Nearly all the officers interviewed also expressed reservations about the increasing powers of the Home Office's new Police Standards Unit, established in July 2002 and already nicknamed the 'provisional wing of HMIC' within ACPO.

Particularly resented by Chief Constables was the Unit's focus on BCUs rather than forces, which they felt undermined their authority and pointed the way to the break-up of existing structures in favour of amalgamated regional forces with loose oversight over BCUs micro-managed directly from Whitehall.

According to the Chief Constable of Hampshire, the Home Office now feels that 'everything coming from a BCU is good, and everything else is bad.' He cited a recent meeting convened by the Home Office to announce new plans for BCUs, to which two representatives from every BCU in the country were invited, but only five chief constables.

It was also pointed out that the Home Office is encouraging Chief Constables to give BCUs control over their own budgets. Currently, the degree to which BCUs manage their own finances varies by force: in some, they have control over everything except numbers of officers at various ranks employed, while in others, Chief Constables continue to dictate spending item by item. Senior officers fear that with fully devolved budgeting BCU Commanders will replace more uniformed officers with civilian specialists, and force headquarters will lose much of their raison d'etre, strengthening the argument for further amalgamations.

The importance of local policing

With the notable exception of Kent (see pp30–32), all the forces interviewed stressed the importance of 'local policing', meaning the maintenance of close, continued contact with the communities being served. This was seen not only as making the police more popular, but as helping them with their job, since detections depend on public cooperation and trust.

The most eloquent advocate for local policing was the Chief Constable of Dyfed Powys, who has used it with startling success in his admittedly quiet, stable and homogenous force area. (Dyfed has the best national detection rate, at 62% [HMIC 2001/2 Inspection], and came out top in Policy Exchange's league table in both 2000-'01 and '01-'02.)

In the Chief Constable's view, police forces are more effective when they coincide with identifiable and self-identifying communities. For this reason, small forces often outperform big ones, despite larger overheads. Examples cited were Gloucestershire, Dorset and Northamptonshire. Large, combined forces such as West Mercia and Thames Valley are in contrast hampered by a lack of cohesion and identity. The assumption, when forces were amalgamated back in the 1970s, that bigger forces would inevitably lead to better, more cost-effective policing had proved false, as HMIC data showed. The Chief Constable's argument is borne out by Policy Exchange's league table, according to which some combined forces (such as Northumbria and Devon and Cornwall) do well compared to their peer groups, whereas others (such as Avon and Somerset and West Mercia) do relatively badly.

Since his appointment in March 2000, Dyfed's Chief Constable has been opening, rather than closing, local police stations. Five new mini-stations or 'police offices' are in the process of being established, taking total station numbers from 46 to 51. The costs involved are small, since they employ one or two constables only, supplemented by volunteers. Premises used include a converted ground-floor local authority flat and frontage leased from shops. There are also plans to share space with fire stations.

The new mini-stations, the Chief Constable felt, are both popular with the public (who like in particular the reappearance of traditional blue police lamps), and an efficient use of resources, since they boost crime reporting, recruitment of special constables, and general police-public contact. Officers, he thought, tend to be attached 'by an umbilical cord' to their stations, so that if stations are large and few it is hard to persuade them to cover an area thoroughly. Mobile stations operating out of specially-equipped vans also have disadvantages, since 'no-one knows where they're going to be at any one time, and they don't seem to engage with the public.'

Dyfed also has a policy of answering, so far as possible, all calls for assistance and investigating all reported crime. In the Chief Constable's view, forces that take the 'professional' approach and 'screen out' certain categories of minor or allegedly unsolvable crime forfeit public trust and support. The neighbouring (combined) force of West Mercia, he complained, refused on principle to investigate minor offences of criminal damage, and instead referred its own crime victims to next-door Dyfed:

> 'When people living in border areas are advised to report issues to the force next door...then the public are entitled to question the use of their funds [Police HQ Carmarthen, 2002].'

> ❝ It's a fudge, a mish-mash that doesn't work ❞

Political accountability

On the question of structures of political accountability, all the officers interviewed acknowledged that the current tripartite system of Chief Constable, Home Office and police authority is unsatisfactory, and showed themselves remarkably open to radical new solutions, such as direct accountability to elected mayors.

Senior officers at the Met suffered especially from unclear, overlapping reporting lines, making it extremely difficult for them to set stable goals and priorities. According to one of them:

> 'At the moment, our governance comprises the Home Secretary, Home Office mandarins, the Metropolitan Police Authority, the Mayor, and now the PM directly [thanks to the government's Safer Streets campaign]...We've got this typical British compromise, a gentleman's agreement that we're all equal. But where's the kickback? It's a fudge, a mish-mash that doesn't work. It's not clear; it's complete and utter madness.'

The previous week he had been called into Downing Street to meet with the prime minister, who was 'laser-beam focused on street crime.' The following day he was

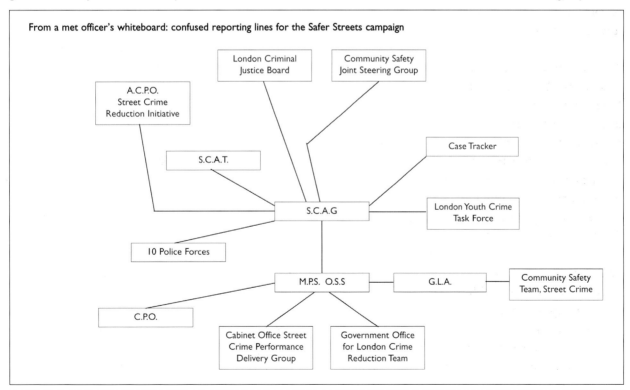

From a met officer's whiteboard: confused reporting lines for the Safer Streets campaign

summoned to the Home Office and asked 'What are you doing on burglary and auto crime, because we've got five-year targets on them.' The result was that 'you've got the PM, the mayor, the PA and the Home Secretary all making different demands. The Met is pulled one way then another...What often happens is that we don't deliver on anything. We do a bit for this person and a bit for that person and don't prioritise [Interview, Territorial Policing HQ 2002].'

It would be better, this officer thought, for the Met to report directly and solely to the Mayor, creating a 'single point of control.' Another advantage of this system would be that the Mayor could also have control over social services, education, transport and housing, and so force cooperation between them and the police. In New York, he noted, Mayor Giuliani often delegated powers over other public services to the police chief, making the chief in effect deputy mayor. It was difficult, however, to see how this could be made to work in London, where borough councils rather than the mayor controlled most public services, and the Mayor's powers were rather limited. Handing control over BCUs to boroughs would not make sense either, because London's criminals operated city-wide, and because manpower had to be re-deployable from one borough to another as crime patterns fluctuated.

A second Met Commander thought the Metropolitan Police Authority too big and unwieldy to exercise effective political oversight, and envisaged the Met being broken down to borough level for regular crime, with more serious crimes being dealt with at the city level. Borough-sized forces would be overseen by directly-elected borough police authorities. Although these authorities might be over-populist initially, the system would be self-correcting. 'In the short term people might say 'Go and chase the pavement-poopers.' But they'd quickly see burglaries going up, and change their minds.' Borough councils in general he regarded as cooperative and sensible: 'The rotten boroughs thing is in the past, at least here in London.'

The chief executive of the high-crime London borough of Southwark worked well with his local borough Commander, but also wanted local government to have more control over the police. In particular, he wanted the power to appoint his own Commander ('at the moment we've got someone very good, but we might not be so lucky next time'), power to top up the Commander's salary if necessary, power to allocate more money to the police ('there's no process whereby we could increase our force from 700 to 800'), and more local recruitment, which would help get more ethnic minorities into uniform but which had histori-cally been avoided because it was perceived to encourage corruption.

Giving local government big new responsibilities would also necessitate, he conceded, substantial local government reforms. Currently, councillors lacked the skills and weight to take on major new tasks. Standing up to senior police officers was particularly difficult:

> 'One, it's the way they dress. Two, they run military-style operations; they're not used to being contradicted. Three, they've got a huge amount of information. Four, they can always say 'But this is a central directive.' '

Similar points were made by Dyfed's Chief Constable and police authority vice-chair. The Major government's reforms to police authorities, in the Chief Constable's view, had stripped them of legitimacy and visibility, damaging local accountability. The Welsh Assembly was now stepping into the vacuum, and had ambitions to take responsibility for all Welsh forces. The vice-chair of the Dyfed police authority was pessimistic about local government in general, pointing out that it was hard to recruit people to local consultative committees because they knew that the real decisions were taken elsewhere, and regarded them as 'wasted time'. This detachment and cynicism represented a 'real malaise'.

Dyfed's Chief Constable (a former Met officer), also

favoured, with reservations, the idea of putting local forces under the control of locally-elected mayors. The public, in his view 'should be allowed to elect the mayor and take the consequences.' But like other officers interviewed he was alarmed at the prospect of forces reporting to controversial figures such as Ray Mallon, the former superintendent elected mayor of Middlesborough in June 2002. Given the three-year criminal investigation of Mallon by Cleveland police and his admission, during internal disciplinary proceedings, that he had offered inducements to suspects in custody, it would be 'almost impossible' to establish a viable police/politician relationship with him. Northern Ireland's notorious 'B Specials' - a Protestant-dominated, part-time volunteer force attached to the Royal Ulster Constabulary before being disbanded in 1970 - was cited by the Chief Constable as an example of the dangers of politicised policing.

Interviewees were remarkably relaxed about the possibility of a redefinition of the principle of constabulary independence. According to officers at the Met, the principle has already been undermined by the 1996 Police Act, which effectively did away with Chief Constables'

managerial autonomy. It was now 'an outdated concept' and 'a fiction', and other legal safeguards meant that 'no politician could force us to do anything illegal.' Dyfed's Chief Constable agreed that operational independence had been much eroded: the sole remaining element of the principle to which he held firm being that 'no man can tell me whom to arrest.'

The Safer Streets Initiative

Introduction

Our UK fieldwork coincided with the government's 'Safer Streets' initiative, launched, amidst much publicity, in March 2002 to combat a sudden upswing in street robberies and muggings. Characterised as a 'national emergency' by the prime minister [HMIC Inspection Report, May 2002], the trend appeared to be driven by improving home security, a squeeze in the casual labour market and growing use of mobile phones [*The Economist*, 23/3/02].

The initiative covered ten forces whose areas were identified as accounting for 82% of all street robberies: the Met, West Midlands, Greater Manchester, Merseyside,

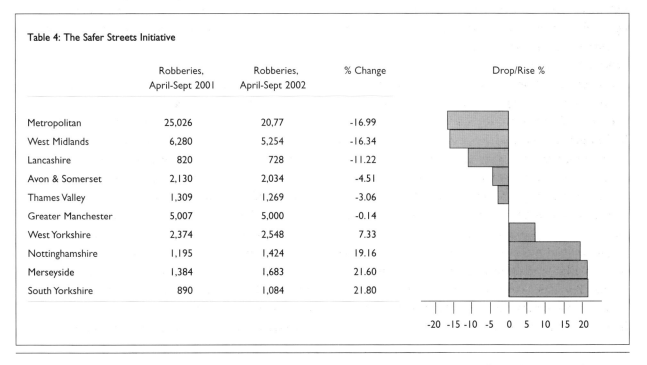

Table 4: The Safer Streets Initiative

	Robberies, April-Sept 2001	Robberies, April-Sept 2002	% Change	Drop/Rise %
Metropolitan	25,026	20,77	-16.99	
West Midlands	6,280	5,254	-16.34	
Lancashire	820	728	-11.22	
Avon & Somerset	2,130	2,034	-4.51	
Thames Valley	1,309	1,269	-3.06	
Greater Manchester	5,007	5,000	-0.14	
West Yorkshire	2,374	2,548	7.33	
Nottinghamshire	1,195	1,424	19.16	
Merseyside	1,384	1,683	21.60	
South Yorkshire	890	1,084	21.80	

-20 -15 -10 -5   0   5   10   15   20

Avon and Somerset, South Yorkshire, West Yorkshire, Nottinghamshire, Thames Valley and Lancashire. It ran from April to September 2002 and cost an estimated £67m, spent chiefly on additional manpower, overtime and information technology.

The initiative was driven from an extremely high level. Administered by the PSU, in the first major test of the new body's effectiveness, it was overseen by a ministerial committee called the Street Crime Action Group (SCAG). Including Cabinet ministers, senior law officers and police, this resembled the cabinet-level committees convened to tackle the Foot and Mouth Disease outbreak, the September 11th crisis and the winter 2002 fire-fighters' strike. The PSU had earlier established a robbery initiative covering the ten forces, and SCAG's Safer Streets campaign effectively took over and expanded this. Ten government ministers were also each assigned a 'failing force', with responsibility to push for quick action and encourage inter-agency working (though in practice, their involvement was rather limited.)

A success or a failure?

When the Safer Streets initiative drew to a close in September, the prime minister hailed it as 'one of the most successful partnerships between government and the police in living memory.' From April to September, street crime had fallen by an average 16% across the ten forces. Compared with same period the previous year, however, the picture looked less rosy. Overall, street crime had fallen by only 10% in the ten force areas, and in four out of the ten areas (West Yorkshire, South Yorkshire, Nottinghamshire and Merseyside), it had actually risen [The Guardian 15/10/02].

In other ways, also, the Safer Streets' achievements are questionable. First, it is not clear that street crime was in fact a major problem for all ten of the participating forces. According to an HMIC assessment a month into the initiative, it was indeed a serious problem for the Met and West Midlands, but other forces 'were candid in their assessment of street crime as a low priority locally', and

when special funding ceased it was 'unlikely that ...activity would continue at anything like its current level [HMIC May 2002].' In the words of a senior Lancashire officer, 'We didn't see street crime as a strategic threat, but if the prime minister tells you it's a problem, then it becomes a problem [Interview, 2002].'

Second, the initiative was extraordinarily expensive. Taking the headline figure of a reduction by 4,618 in the number of robberies in the ten force areas over the life of the Safer Streets, and a total Safer Streets spend of £67m, it cost a startling £14,508 per crime prevented [Police Review, 18/10/02].

Third, Safer Streets used a great deal of manpower, diverting it from arguably equally or more important tasks. According to HMIC, nominated Assistant Chief Constables spent 50%-60% of their time managing the campaign, assisted by a Superintendent and small management team. Forces generally dedicated between 1% and 8% of their full-time staff to the initiative altogether. Resources were thus diverted away from other crimes and less street-crime prone areas, often against the will of local police authorities:

> 'It is acknowledged that resourcing the initiative pulls experienced resources from other operational areas of policing, leaving a higher proportion of probationers. In some forces this has produced a significant element of the 'front line' of policing being carried out by the least experienced personnel. Additionally, in those forces where street crime is not a force wide problem, the removal of staff from unaffected areas is the subject of increasing concern, especially amongst elected representatives on the police authority' [HMIC May 2002: 3.3.3/4].

In South Yorkshire half the Safer Streets staff (about 30 people), were taken from the traffic division, leaving it without the manpower to cover anything except fatal accidents. Road deaths rose during the life of the campaign, and the inspection of heavy goods vehicles for compliance with environmental and health and safety laws virtually ceased [Interview, 2002].'

Fourth, the prime minister's vague blanket target of bringing street crime 'under control' by the end of September took no account of differing patterns and causes of street crime in different force areas. HMIC's preliminary report noted, for example, that whereas in London and elsewhere street crime was largely committed by delinquent teenagers, in Bristol (covered by Avon and Somerset), it was a by-product of a 'drugs market focused around crack cocaine and Jamaican criminals.' [HMIC 2002:3:1.4]. HMIC was also concerned that Safer Streets took no account of community tensions in West Yorkshire, which had suffered ethnic riots the previous summer.

As a result, perhaps, of these regional differences, Safer Streets was much less successful in some police force areas than in others. Though in best-performing London robbery fell by 17%, in worst-performing South Yorkshire and Merseyside it rose 22%.

The view from the ground

These problems and more were reflected in interviews. In Nottinghamshire, an officer complained that street robbery only accounted for only 2,700 out of 150,000 recorded offences over the previous twelve months, or less than 2% of the area's total crime. '13,000 burglaries and countless traffic offences' were 'now being sidelined.' Nor, according to consultations with local government and community representatives under the 1998 Crime and Disorder Act, was street crime something the citizens of Nottinghamshire were particularly worried about: it 'didn't come up in a single crime audit.' Thanks to a rash of mobile phone snatches in London, Nottinghamshire was being forced to abandon local initiatives planned with locally-elected representatives in favour of an unnecessary scheme dictated by Whitehall:

'What makes it worse is that on the first of April we rolled out a new partnership strategy, cutting

divisions from 5 to 4 and giving co-terminosity with other boundaries. Computer costs, shift systems, staff locations which took two years to reorganize have gone by the board.' [Interview, 2002]

Elsewhere, senior officers were concerned at the way in which Safer Streets added to the powers of the PSU. Its head, Kevin Bond, had such large funds at his disposal and interfered with operational matters, including the acquisition of expensive information technology, to such an extent that he had 'become the Chief Constable.' They also distrusted central government's short-termism and over-sensitivity to the media. At weekly meetings of SCAG's operational sub-committee, according to one officer, 'a 6% fall in street crime made them ecstatic, and a 6% rise made them apoplectic', despite the obvious impossibility of judging crime trends on one week's returns.

Conclusions

The Safer Streets campaign is a textbook case of the drawbacks of centralised policing. Though it succeeded in modestly reducing street crime in some areas, it did so at enormous cost, diverted resources away from other policing tasks, and undermined local accountability mechanisms and partnerships between local forces and other local public services.

Despite this, the government appears keen to launch more centralised policing initiatives. The Home Secretary's first National Policing Plan, published in November 2002 under the provisions of the new Police Reform Act, details 51 'actions' that chief officers and police authorities must take into account when formulating local policing plans [Home Office 2002: 44-48]. Of the 51, 19 include specific targets, some to be achieved on average nationwide, others to be achieved force by force. These range from a target 25% fewer domestic burglaries by 2005, to a 15% reduction in overtime spend by 2006, to 40% fewer road deaths and injuries by 2010. The ten forces involved with Safer Streets must 'maintain momentum' so as to have reduced robbery by 14% by 2005.

The Kent Policing Model

Introduction

Developed by Kent Constabulary in the mid 1990s, the Kent Policing Model (KPM) is an example of a policing strategy that despite having been developed by a local force, is unpopular with much of the public. Described as 'intelligence-led policing', it seeks to analyse crime patterns systematically and objectively, and allocate resources accordingly. In practice, this means that it concentrates resources on serious crime and known criminals, at the expense of general policing, and especially traditional foot patrols. Developed and promoted by Kent's Chief Constable (currently also president of ACPO), it has won the approval of HMIC and the Home Secretary, as detailed in his November 2002 National Policing Plan. Under the title 'National Intelligence Model', it is due to be implemented by all forces by April 2004.

> " it may not be what the public wants, but it's what it needs "

What is the KPM?

Under the KPM, crime is divided into three. 'Level one' crime is unplanned, unsophisticated and restricted to a specific locale. 'Level two' crime is committed by professional, trans-regional criminals and includes burglary, auto-theft, handling of stolen goods and medium-scale drug-dealing. Level three crime is national and transnational, and includes people-trafficking, international fraud and drug-dealing, organised paedophilia and the distribution of pornography on the internet.

In the absence of such categorisation, supporters of the Kent model argue, 'level two' criminals operating across police force borders are often ignored. These typically include burglars targeting old people, regional drug syndicates and serial sex offenders. The KPM, in contrast, stresses the importance of detective units in tracking and bringing to book these middle-tier criminals.

A necessary corollary of KPM is that policing priorities are not chosen, in the words of a Kent officer, 'in response to the public's perception of crime or public demand.' One of its 'basic requirements' is a programme 'to educate the community' as to what constitutes a crime problem, and to change the public's perception of what the police will do. Though the KPM, according to this officer 'may not be what the public wants, it's what it needs [Interview, Police HQ Maidstone, 2002].'

A success or a failure?

The Kent police have performed reasonably well since the introduction of the KPM in 1995. From 1995-2002 recorded crime in the force area fell 22% (slightly more than the national average fall of 19%), and detection rates are slightly better than the national average. According to Policy Exchange's league table of the forty-two English and Welsh police forces, Kent also scores well compared with forces covering comparable areas, doing better than all other forces save Hampshire in the group of eleven 'rich suburban' force areas.

Though the Kent Constabulary's recent performance has been good, it is nonetheless clear that its policing model has some serious drawbacks.

First, its emphasis on detective-led intelligence work drains uniformed divisions, especially patrols and response teams, of manpower and resources, as well as prestige. As HMIC noted in a 1997-'98 report:

'The demands of the KPM do not diminish the requirement to maintain an effective patrol function...KPM can have a detrimental effect on the self-esteem of patrolling officers, and a number during this Inspection raised their continued perception - wrongheaded as it may be - that their patrolling role is insufficiently recognised . . . Implementation of the demand management strategy...would alleviate the reduction in patrol strength arising out of the transfer of patrol officers into specialist KPM units [HMIC 1997/98:3.41].'

Kent's most recent HMIC Inspection report (2001/02) was complimentary, but also noted that the transfer of resources away from general policing and into detection had led to 'low levels of victim satisfaction, delayed attention being given to some crime reports, and investigative officers being overburdened by the sheer numbers of reports allocated to them.' Kent was also criticised for failing to record crime. In 2000 it introduced 'assault clinics', to which crime reports were passed from a central call centre and at which victims were supposed to be interviewed and offences logged. In practice, HMIC noted, four in ten crime victims failed to attend assault clinics, with the result that many crimes telephoned in to call centres were never officially recorded. This was not in accordance with the new National Crime Recording Standard (NCRS), and a 'more rigorous' and 'victim-oriented' system was needed.

Second and most importantly, the KPM does not, according to interviews with elected representatives, command the confidence of the public. According to a Kent councillor, while the KPM may have reduced major crime, it has not reduced fear of crime. He knew from numerous local consultation meetings that the public were worried 'that there are no police around any more, and that they don't seem to respond to small incidents.' This was due to the fact that officers no longer worked their own neighbourhoods, but shared responsibility for much larger districts, alienating them from the communities they served. He also fielded frequent complaints about falling numbers of patrol officers. At parish council meetings, this was 'always the big issue.'

Though personally in favour of 'intelligence-led policing', he felt community-based 'reassurance policing' to be equally important, especially since a visit to a US police department, which demonstrated that a community-based approach, using Community Service Officers and Rangers alongside full police officers, could successfully cut crime. He regularly raised these topics with Kent Police:

'18 months ago we finally decided to pay for more police officers ourselves. We set up 12 community wardens and 12 police officers to patrol local villages. It was the only way we could get what we wanted [Interview, Shire Hall, Maidstone 2002].'

The number of council-funded community wardens is due to grow to 100 over the next four years. In exchange, the Chief Constable has funded an extra 62 officers, and 24 new jointly-badged police cars out of his own budget.

Two weeks after the launch of this £2.5m initiative, the Chief Constable defended the Kent Policing Model at ACPO's annual conference, condemning the idea that a situation where 'all the officers are known to all the community' could be recreated as 'an impossible Enid Blyton scenario.' He also criticised the Home Secretary's enthusiasm for auxiliary police or Community Support Officers (CSOs), saying that he saw 'little merit in CSOs...It seems to me the money would be better spent on more police officers [*The Times* 14/5/02.].'

The county council's concerns were echoed at the district level. Again, interviewees complained that intelligence-led policing meant that officers operated over much wider areas, distancing them from local communities. The model diverted resources away from minor crime: though an area might suffer a great deal of 'petty vandalism, burglary and thefts from gardens', the KPM rated them 'not important enough for permanent police cover.' Often, the KPM did not tackle acknowledged 'hotspots' either:

'The Edenbridge overspill estates are a hot spot. There's a lot of drug-dealing, and shop owners were being terrorised by a small group of kids, with one owner being threatened with no insurance renewal as a result. The Edenbridge Town Forum sent a strong letter [to the Chief Constable], asking for police cover. The local commander met them and said that the problem was getting witnesses so that they could prosecute. But it was clear that it was because the police weren't there that people were frightened and didn't feel protected. Just a police presence would have been sufficient deterrence [Interview, Sevenoaks District Council, 2002].'

The public, this councillor reported, also much disliked the closure of local police stations, and their replacement with a call centre at Maidstone. Often, call centre staff had never heard of the place from which crime victims were calling, and it was now 'taking longer for

> **The KPM isn't intelligence-led policing, it's invisible policing**

the police to turn up.' Similarly, a Kent Member of Parliament worried that local stations 'rooted in the community, are dying out', and that 'in village after village the middle classes are turning against the police.' The Kent Policing Model, in his view, was not 'intelli-

gence-led policing, but invisible policing [Interview, M. Fallon MP, 2002].'

A member of Medway council agreed that in her district, 'policing is so covert that you don't even know it exists.' She was strongly against proposals to close Rochester, Gillingham and Chatham police stations, and wanted a new station at Strood, which was the gateway from London to the Medway towns, and which suffered growing numbers of muggings and armed robberies. The low priority given quite major crime - on Rochester High Street, for example, one could 'buy drugs in any pub', and taxi drivers refused to go there at night - was in her view 'appalling.' A second Medway councillor was less critical of the Kent Policing Model, considering that changing crime patterns required new techniques, and that it would, once bedded in, work well. She conceded, however, that Kent Constabulary's public relations were 'dire':

> 'Historically, the job of the police was simply to uphold the law, and beyond that they didn't have to account for their actions. If, for example, they didn't respond to a call there was no need to apologise. But things have changed - we've got a complaints culture now, and people are ready to criticise. Kent is taking some time to get used to the idea [Interview, Medway District Council, 2002].'

Medway, like the county council, had responded to public demand for more uniformed local policing by paying for it itself. The council paid overtime for six

officers, using them to patrol problem areas such as Rochester High Street. It also employed six civilian Wardens (one paid for by the Medway Housing Society), who patrolled in pairs after three months' training. Medway planned to expand the scheme, and saw itself as 'in a sense going down the French route towards municipal policing.'

Conclusion - an accountability gap

The merits of the Kent Policing Model as a policing strategy are debatable. What it does illustrate, however, is forces' lack of accountability to local communities. Councillors and MPs interviewed were unanimous in their frustration at not being able to influence policing in response to the express wishes of their electors, and in many cases advocated radical new systems of police force oversight.

An MP felt that there was 'no local accountability at all', and that he was 'completely unable to influence what's actually provided on the ground.' On station closures, for example, there had been 'no dialogue with the Chief Constable, who just gives us quarterly forty-minute talks, which aren't very helpful.' Recently, he was surprised to learn that a decision had been taken to build a multi-million firearms range for the Kent police, and wondered if this was part of the policing plan worked out with the council. As an MP, he had 'no contact' with the police authority. (In the words of another MP, 'I neither know nor care who the chair of the police authority in my constituency is. It's of no importance.') In his view, elected mayors should be put in charge of police, and he was 'even coming round to the idea that commanders should be selected by local residents, and that the council should be able to haul them up to explain what they're doing.' For this to work, local authorities had to have control over police funding, and perhaps also be able to raise a police tax. Implications for constabulary independence did not worry him, since ACPO had already turned itself into 'a division of the Home Office.'

Councillors expressed similar views. The current system, in one interviewee's view, was 'cheating the people. They don't ask for much, and what they do ask for isn't unreasonable.' Twenty years' experience had convinced her that 'any idea that the Kent police know what the public need is nonsense.' Police authorities were ineffective: 'the police authority exists, but I don't get much information about it, and don't know how to influence it. They're rather like health trusts - full of appointees.' Again, she was unconcerned about the principle of constabulary independence, which was 'nothing more than a convenient excuse [for inaction].'

As another councillor put it, the only way he can influence the way Kent is policed is 'by the use of money', and that despite the presence of elected members on the police authority, it is 'basically a police vehicle to take the budget through.' He felt that the Conservative government's police authority reforms of the mid-'90s had been a mistake, and that all authority members should be elected, 'especially the chairman.' Even better, Chief Constables could be made directly accountable to council leaders.

3. The United States

How Policing Works in the US

Introduction

In the United States, policing is delivered, managed and financed locally. Each US county can set up its own police department. This is a constitutional right (by state charter), and it is no surprise that most choose to do so. The system is therefore heavily decentralised and fragmented. This has a number of implications. First, it gives local politicians control over the strategic direction of policing. Second, it gives rise to wide variations in policing methods due to differing local government structures, political agendas and tax bases. Third, the system encourages police forces to be strongly accountable to the public, and responsive to public demands.

There are three layers of policing in the US: federal, state and local.[5] In total, there are about 18,760 separate police agencies. They employ nearly one million law enforcement personnel, and spend a combined annual budget of about $51 billion. At the federal level, there are about sixty different agencies (for example the Federal Bureau of Investigation, U.S. Marshals and the Secret Service). At the state level, a variety of police forces exist (for example, the Highway Patrol, in 26 states, and State Police, in 23 states).

Federal Law Enforcement agencies with national responsibilities are funded directly. In addition, about $4 billion per annum of federal money is distributed to local law enforcement bodies across the country. This goes to courts and correctional facilities as well as to police. However, local police forces receive the vast bulk of their funding from local sales and property taxes, a typical split being about 80% local funding versus 20% federal. The system means that different forces enjoy significantly different levels of funding. This translates into a wide variation in the amount of spending per head of population ($554 per resident in Washington DC down to $94 per head in El Paso [2000 figures, from Bureau of Justice Statistics Bulletin, February 2002]).

An example of a jurisdiction with funding constraints is the City of Philadelphia. With a limited tax base, this

Table 5: Policing structures in the United States			
	Federal	State	Local
Annual spend($65.4 billion total)[6]	$14.7 billion(21 %)	$9.6 billion(14 %)	$45.5 billion(65 %)
Agencies	60 Agencies(mainly clustered in the Justice Department or Treasury Department.)	Several hundred agencies	Over 15,000 municipal agencies. About 3,100 county sheriff's offices.

Source: http:// faculty.ncwc.edu/toconnor/polstruct.htm

relatively poor authority is constantly forced to make hard choices between different public services. Resources for the City Police Department have always been limited, restricting what the force can realistically achieve. In Philadelphia, the spend per resident was $253 (in 2000), putting it in the middle of the budget range for cities of over a million residents. However, its spend per sworn employee was a mere $55,000 - the lowest figure out of America's ten biggest cities.

Local control over police forces also means that different areas of the US pursue radically different policing policies. Levels of service and service priorities cannot be dictated centrally. Though the federal government can encourage local forces to adopt its initiatives by offering funding, it cannot compel local forces adopt them. One recent example is the 'Community Oriented Policing Scheme' (COPS), initiated by President Clinton in January 1994. By 1997, $1.4 billion was being spent by federal government on the programme annually, but there was no clear evidence that this had translated into an actual increase in police numbers on the ground [Muhlhausen 2002]. When local forces do adopt new initiatives, they are much likelier to copy other forces' successes, such as New York Police Department's (NYPD) Compstat model (see pp40–43).

The organisation of local forces

The US has two types of local police force: municipal and county. County police departments are often headed by an elected sheriff (of whom there are about 3,100). Larger counties generally have a chief of police, appointed by local politicians to lead the police department. Municipal police departments, of which there are over 15,000, include transit, school and housing police. These range in size from the largest, New York (with about 40,000 officers) to the smallest (800 municipal police forces consist of only a single officer). The vast majority have 10 or fewer officers. The box below shows Utah's disposition of state, county and municipal departments.

Systems of political accountability

Regardless of the specific local government and police force structure in any given district, the principle of local political accountability remains. In the small town of Medical Lake, Washington, for example, the police chief reports to the mayor and city administrator. In Hampden, Massachusetts, a town of 5,100, the police chief reports to a three-member board, while in the city of Fountain, Colorado, the chief reports to a city manager.

The main features of the US's localised, politically-driven policing system are:
- strong strategic, verging into operational, direction from the mayor, city council or elected sheriff, because their re-election depends on delivery;
- powers to local politicians to set police budgets and funding priorities; and
- in the mayor's case, powers to hire and fire the chief of police.

Table 6: Utah police departments

State	County	Municipal
Utah(650 officers)	Duchesne Co. Sheriff's office (120 officers)	Moab(15 officers)
	Emery Co. Sheriff's office(100 officers)	Ogden(350 officers)
	Salt Lake Co. Sheriff's office(350 officers)	Provo(325 officers)
		Salt Lake City(1,000 officers)

Source: www.dps.state.ut.us

Mayors

Around 44% of US cities operate under a mayor-council model [International City/County Management Association, 2002]. This comprises an elected legislature (the council) and a separately elected executive (the mayor). In several cities, including New York and Detroit, the mayor also appoints a 'police commissioner' or, as in Los Angeles, a board of commissioners. The role of the commissioner is to oversee and audit the police and to help handle police discipline and complaints.

Mayors' powers generally include the ability to hire and fire police chiefs. Lower level officers enjoy civil service employment rights and the mayor is not allowed to intervene in recruitment or promotion decisions.

Mayors have the power to set the police force's budget. However, the budget usually has to be approved by the council. This can lead to stalemate. In Chicago in the late 1980s the Democrats lost the mayoralty but retained a majority on the council. This resulted in weeks of wrangling over the budget, which only ended at five to midnight on December 31st because Illinois State law required the city to have a budget in place by January 1st. This, however, is an extreme case and one interviewee told us that 'in the US there is a fairly continuous process of negotiation between the two ends of city hall, much as there often is between the two ends of Pennsylvania Avenue'.

City/County Managers

All US cities have mayors, but larger cities and counties, with more complicated public administration needs, commonly also employ city managers, appointed by the mayor or city council. The first such post was established in Staunton, Virginia, in 1908, and today there are just over 3,000 of them across the US. Research suggests that cities with them are better run than those without [Segal and Moore 2002]. In half of all American cities, direct responsibility for appointing the police chief and setting the budget for the police now lies with the manager and not the mayor [Interview, E. Lehrer, AEI, Washington DC 2002]. This reduces the political flavour of these decisions.

Police chiefs

Municipal and county police departments are led by a chief officer. In most cases, chief officers are appointed, but in some they are directly or indirectly elected. Appointed police chiefs report to either a mayor, a city manager, or to a board appointed by the mayor or legislature. In general, chief officers are hired on a 'three year hire and no tenure' basis. Most chiefs manage around two years in post, before moving on or being replaced [Interview, NIJ, Washington DC, 2002]. Their employment contracts universally state that they hold office 'at the pleasure of the mayor' (or county board), creating a clear line of authority and accountability.

Police chiefs are often brought in to 'fix' specific problems. A recent example was the October 2002 appointment of William Bratton as chief of police in Los Angeles. The mayor of Los Angeles, James Hahn, brought him in as a response to civil rights violations by the Los Angeles Police Department (LAPD). In July 2002 there was public and media criticism of the department following the videotaped beating of a black teenager by police. Bratton's tenure will depend on his performance: he is expected to succeed, 'or explain why' [Interview, NIJ, Washington DC 2002].

One of the major constraints on police chiefs are labour laws. They vary from state to state, with the result that the terms and conditions of police employment vary widely. Within a 'labor town' like Philadelphia more job protection is provided than in some other cities. Here, according to an interviewee, achieving detective rank 'effectively means retirement'; a former chief of Philadelphia police could not be blamed for failing to reduce crime in the city, because without powers to hire or fire he 'didn't have the tools to do the job [Interview, R.E. Moffet, Heritage Foundation, Washington DC, 2002].' In Virginia, by contrast, the State does not accept collective bargaining and police pay is determined on the basis of the pay rates for comparative police forces.

The politicisation of US policing: strengths and drawbacks

The strength of the American system of politically accountable local policing is its responsiveness to local needs and demands, as transmitted via locally-elected leaders with power over appointments and budgets. A vivid example of this is provided by Philadelphia, where a strong, pro-active mayor has forced the police to tackle drug-dealing on the streets effectively. As a policy advisor to the police chief puts it:

'Our current mayor, John F. Street, is strong and has clear ideas about reducing crime. He didn't know anything about crime [when he took office in 2000], but told the chief of police that he wanted it cut. The current chief, Sylvester Johnson, isn't as strong as his predecessor Chief Timoney, who came down from NYPD, and it now sometimes feels like the mayor is second-guessing him. The Narcotics Unit used to target the big drugs traffickers, but the mayor said he wanted the streets to be targeted instead, because the public wanted something done. All the street corners in the city used by drug sellers - about 300 of them - had to be allocated 2 police officers day and night to stop the sales. This is now the strategy, with all the overtime costs being paid for directly by the mayor.'

The strategy was a success:

'Now that the streets have been cleared of dealers, people are using them again. There have even been street parties! But the fact is that it was the mayor who demanded this approach; it was he who saw that drug-dealing had become a quality-of-life issue [Interview, G Wasserman Philadelphia PD HQ 2002].'

US-style politicised policing does, however, also have major drawbacks. Most importantly, the interdependence of local politicians and senior police officers can encourage corruption: a police chief dependent on a mayor for re-appointment might not be zealous in investigating allegations of bribe-taking in the mayor's office, for instance. There have been several notorious cases of this sort, not least the scandals emanating from the office of Washington DC Mayor Marion Barry in the late 1980s. Barry was the target of several federal probes into alleged corruption before finally being brought down when videotaped smoking crack-cocaine in an FBI-run sting operation in January 1990.

A report by Transparency International [Transparency International, March 2002] details the dangers and remedies, highlighting long histories of local corruption in Providence, Rhode Island; Camden, New Jersey, Chicago and Los Angeles.

In Providence, one governor, two local mayors, three judges, a councilman and three directors of public works were convicted of racketeering, extortion, converting state money to personal use, obtaining money under false pretences, obstructing justice and improper campaign-finance reporting between 1987 and 1998. In the summer of 2002 the current mayor of Providence, Vincent 'Buddy' Cianci, was convicted of conspiring to solicit bribes for city contracts and sentenced to five years' imprisonment. Five other city officials, (including the chair and vice-chair of the tax board, Cianci's director of administration and his chief of staff), and five local businessmen and lawyers have also been indicted on racketeering charges. Importantly, the three-year operation that eventually nailed Cianci and his associates was initiated and led not by Providence's police force, but by the FBI, and the resulting prosecutions took place in federal rather than state courts. Rhode Island's own statutory ethics code and Ethics Commission have not, in Transparency International's view, 'been a force...in the fight against corruption.'

Camden, New Jersey presents a similar picture, with three of its last five mayors having been convicted on corruption charges while in office. The latest of these figures, Mayor Michael Milan, was convicted in 2000 of taking bribes from contractors, associating with mob figures, concealing a loan from a drug-dealer and staging a burglary for the purpose of insurance fraud. Sixteen others were convicted with him. Again, the investigation into the mayor's office was led by the FBI rather than the local police, and the FBI actually excluded the police once they began to suspect that they were alerting suspects to upcoming raids. These suspicions grew following the conviction of the local detective who worked as Milan's personal bodyguard, and the wiretapping of conversations between a local drugs baron and two police officers. New Jersey's Executive Commission on Ethical Standards and Camden County's own ethics board signally failed either to prevent or investigate the whole affair.

More common than corrupt mayors are weak ones, who let police forces get out of control. A high-profile example was Thomas Bradley of Los Angeles, who clashed with LAPD chief Daryl Gates following the public beating of a black suspect, Rodney King, by white police officers in March 1991. Shielded by an ineffectual part-time Board of Police Commissioners, Gates refused Bradley's request to resign [Woods 1993:284]. An independent commission set up to investigate the case recommended that in future the chief of police should be required to be more responsive to LA's elected leadership.

It proposed that the police chief should be appointed by the mayor with the consent of the council 'after an open competition' and should serve a single 5 year term renewable for one additional term at the police commission's discretion. It also recommended that the commission should be able to terminate the chief's contract at any time with the mayor's agreement, but that the termination should be reversible by a two-thirds vote of the city council [Woods 1993:288/9].

Though these reforms were implemented in 1993-1994, the LAPD's problems persisted. In the course of the 1998-2000 'Rampart' corruption scandal over seventy anti-gang unit officers were accused of drug-dealing, perjury, and the planting of 'drop guns' on unarmed civilians. Civil suits brought on the back of the scandal have so far cost Los Angeles over $25m, and the eventual total settlement costs are estimated at $125m. A Board of Inquiry into the affair convened by the LAPD police chief was conservative in its recommendations, but a 190-strong Review Panel formed by the police commission was more robust, criticising the commission for weak oversight of the LAPD, and the mayor's office for obstructionism.

Transparency International's conclusion from all these cases is that political corruption at the local level is

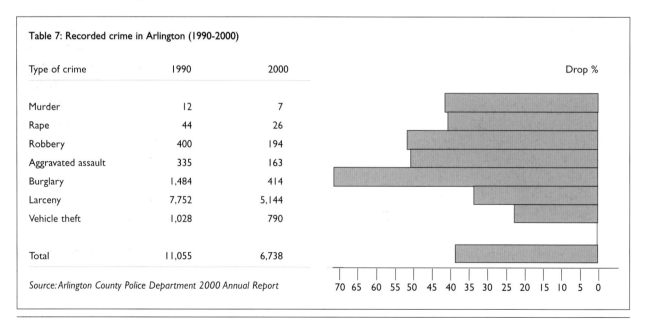

Table 7: Recorded crime in Arlington (1990-2000)

Type of crime	1990	2000	Drop %
Murder	12	7	
Rape	44	26	
Robbery	400	194	
Aggravated assault	335	163	
Burglary	1,484	414	
Larceny	7,752	5,144	
Vehicle theft	1,028	790	
Total	11,055	6,738	

Source: Arlington County Police Department 2000 Annual Report

'widespread' in the USA, and that 'outside-state agencies' are needed to prosecute it. Local audit institutions are only effective if genuinely independent from city hall, and properly staffed and funded. Vital too are independent, vigorous and serious local newspapers [Transparency International 2002: 28-32].'

Policing in Arlington, Virginia

One of the most successful examples of the localised model of policing is Arlington County, Virginia. While there has been a general fall in crime across the US, the results in Arlington are particularly impressive.

Arlington has a five person county board and was one of the first to introduce the post of county manager. The identity of the county manager tends to reflect the political priorities of the majority and the police chief (who like the county manager serves at the pleasure of the board) is expected to apply the board and the manager's policing philosophy. The average tenure for a police chief in Arlington is 'around 5 years'.

> " the public are paying for the service "

The Arlington police department (PD) is small - just 362 officers. Its internal ratings are good - with a majority of Arlington county residents assessing the performance and the overall competency of PD employees as 'very good' [Arlington PD: 2000]. Residents particularly value police patrol and public contact [Annual Report 2000:36/37]. With a large population, and borders with both Maryland and Pennsylvania, violent crime can be a problem. The department is heavily committed to an 'immediate response' to calls and aims for a 2 minute response time. It takes a particularly consumerist view - 'the public are paying for the service so they should get the service they want'.

For the Arlington police, 'good policing' means that patrol officers develop close links with their local area. Most officers are posted to a single district location for seven years. This means that they are able to establish and sustain a close association with the community and build a positive relationship with it. This in turn enables the police to provide public reassurance and gather in-depth information about the neighbourhood which helps them combat crime.

There is no canteen provision, which means that the police are always out and about. Within the county, there are mostly one-man patrols in cars. A proportion of the total force is assigned to the detective bureau - but never more than 10 percent (35 to 40 officers). Over 170 officers remain in uniform, providing a visible, local police presence. The relatively small size of the department is not viewed as impeding its operational efficiency or co-operation with neighbouring forces. There are regular operations that cross police borders, and a number of 'mutual aid agreements' with surrounding police departments. [Interview, Arlington PD 2002].

Policing in New York City

The success of the New York Police Department has been widely covered [Silverman 1999; Maple 1999]. Nevertheless, the basic details are worth repeating. A decade ago New York faced an unparalleled homicide rate: in 1993 1,946 men women and children were murdered in New York City. As a result, crime in general and gun crime in particular became leading issues in the campaign for New York mayor that year. The winner, Mayor Rudi Giuliani, began by appointing a new commissioner, William Bratton, who as chief of the New York transit police had won a reputation for cracking down on previously ignored beggars and fare-dodgers.

As head of police for New York City, Bratton adopted a novel policy position, supported and financed by Giuliani. He argued that 'quality of life' issues mattered to city residents, and should therefore matter to the NYPD. He instituted a major reorganisation of the department, spelling the end of many of the numerous specialist units and squads. He also introduced a computerised data-collection system that allowed the department to break down crime statistics street by street. This enabled precincts to direct their resources to those areas where crime rates were highest. 'Computer Statistics' (or 'Compstat' as it is now better known), provided an important management tool. For the first time, senior and middle police managers began to have some grasp of precisely what their officers were doing, and the outcomes that followed.

A sense of Bratton's approach in New York can be gained from comments he made following his appointment to the Los Angeles Police Department (LAPD) in October 2002:

'I was amazed to find that out of the 9,000 people
in the police department not a single one focused
on graffiti. As a result you look like the graffiti
capital of the world. I would like to focus on that
issue because it reflects community pride. It reflects
a sense of caring'.

In Los Angeles he plans a rapid reconfiguration of the department's specialised units such as robbery, homicide, narcotics, and gang divisions. In his words, 'my own sense of the Police Department is that it is an overspecialised, compartmentalised department. The LAPD is policing the 1950s.' [Los Angeles Times 10/10/02]

At the NYPD, Bratton similarly fundamentally reordered policing priorities. The thrust of the Bratton reforms in policing was to return control of the department to the uniformed arm by placing immediate responsibility for crime on the shoulders of uniformed precinct captains.

Initially, police attention and resources were directed towards homicide and gun crime. However, there was a simultaneous concern for quality of life issues, which served to heighten the role and status of uniform patrol officers

within the department. The new focus on fighting crime replaced earlier concerns about 'minimising scandals, maintaining community well-being and preserving a low police profile' [Silverman 1996:10]. The police were instead expected to adopt a much more pro-active approach.

Although the description of Bratton's strategy as 'zero tolerance' policing is incorrect, it did indeed encompass a new commitment to encouraging the use of public space by city residents. At its heart was the aim of reducing fear of victimization. It reflected growing interest in what has become known as the 'Broken Windows' theory, which stresses the effect of minor criminal damage on long-term crime and perceptions of public safety. Other quality of life issues include graffiti, and the ability to use the sidewalks unimpeded by street gangs, prostitutes or panhandlers.

Innovation in New York: the Compstat system

NYPD's development of the 'Compstat' information and resource allocation tool shows how local political control and accountability liberate innovative management.

The NYPD introduced Compstat in April 1994, six months after Giuliani's election and five after Bratton's appointment as chief of police. It allows officers to engage in weekly, monthly and annual crime analysis, broken down by precinct and crime type, using real-time statistics. These are discussed at weekly meetings attended by about 100 officers, including all senior ranks and by lower-ranked officers if responsible for particular initiatives. The mayor can attend as of right; other non-police officials by invitation only.

The permanent Compstat unit consists of 20-30 civilian and sworn officers, who put together information from individual precincts, using a computer database system. Initially, as an officer involved in its launch remembers, the unit was:

'self-taught. We started by putting pins in maps of
the precinct according to offence type and location.
Then we bought software off-the-shelf from a local

computer store, so the implementation costs were minimal. They decided to open Compstat meetings to other agencies early on, so the district attorney and the police chief would often appear - as did the mayor, on occasion [Interview, K. Costello, Office of the Chief of Dept., NYPD 2002].'

Prior to Compstat's introduction, the NYPD relied on FBI crime statistics, which were often six months in arrears:

'Precinct commanders usually did not know a great deal about either the pattern or nature of crime in their precinct. They were much more concerned about 'management matters', which might include complaints from the public concerning their officers; overtime payments and perhaps accidents involving police vehicles. They didn't look at crime reports [Interview, K Costello, NYPD 2002].'

The same point is made by Mayor Giuliani in his memoirs:

'The main frustration with the state of policing was that each set of statistics was already obsolete by the time it was available. Examining the numbers annually or even quarterly wasn't accomplishing anything in real time. By the time a pattern of crime was noticed it would have changed, and when the statistics finally did come in...they didn't reflect the actual volume' [because many crimes were never reported to or recorded by the police] [Giuliani 2002:73].

Compstat, in contrast, is both timely and detailed, encouraging police to focus on crime-fighting rather than administration, and on specific crime hot-spots.

The logistics of Compstat are straightforward. Crime and performance statistics are collected at precinct level, and fed weekly to the permanent Compstat HQ. The data are then used to produce a twelve-page summary of crime statistics, drawn up by senior officers from across the department. The summary feeds into a pre-Compstat meeting attended by the most senior officers in the department, and into a full, three-hour Compstat meeting the following day.

Compstat meetings act as a form of internal audit, allowing senior officers to cross-question juniors in detail on developments in their area. They may choose to concentrate on a few precincts only, or to run through all of them then hone in on two or three during the last hour. No subjects, from the most serious to the most trivial, are out of bounds.

Much use is made of graphics and photographs, projected onto large screens behind the speaker's head. A precinct commander claiming successfully to have rid his district of prostitution, for example, might discover himself standing in front of a photograph, taken by the Compstat unit the previous evening, of girls soliciting on one of 'his' street corners.

At a Compstat meeting for the Bronx borough in August 2002, District 11 (Transit Police) reported a rise in robberies on trains. When asked twice by the chief of police for analysis of the robberies rather than limited descriptions of the incidents, the Head of Transit was unable to answer, and immediately stood down from the podium. This was a humiliation for this senior officer, who later apologised for the 'lapse'. At the next Compstat, she was told, she would be 'first up', and if she failed to give a better account of the problem, would be relocated [Compstat meeting for Bronx borough, Command and Control Centre, Police HQ NYPD, August 2002].

As pointed out by Giuliani in his memoirs, 'even in a highly unionised workforce like the NYPD there is plenty of leverage available. Anyone above the rank of inspector...can be demoted...And those below the management rank can be reassigned - a police officer who lived in Westchester might find himself stationed on Staten Island [Giuliani 2002:72].' Compstat also provides a high-visibility opportunity to praise successful officers and initiatives, and to hand out merit and bravery awards.

The process has increased the responsibilities and the status of uniformed officers, and in particular of precinct commanders. It also forces the uniformed and detective branches to work together:

> 'Within the precinct the commander calls the shots, since it's him who has to answer for it to Compstat. In the past, detectives did what they thought was important, but their work was often not coordinated with the rest of the precinct. That doesn't happen any more, because now the detective bureau works for the precinct and not for itself. It's the street cop who covers the area, and sometimes it's the street cops who'll get more narcotics arrests than the narcotics division. They have local knowledge and information which the 'Narcs' don't have. Another benefit is the opportunity Compstat gives for junior officers to talk directly to the most senior officers in NYPD' [Interview, Capt H Knoor, NYPD Police Plaza 2002].

The Compstat approach percolates down through the precinct to the platoon level, forcing precinct commanders to keep in close communication with their subordinates. Junior officers can also be required to attend the full Compstat and to present information or provide explanations to the chiefs of divisions and the Commissioner. Compstat thus creates a weekly interface between top management and operational officers on the ground [K. Costello, NYPD 2002].

Though Compstat involves the collection of statistics, NYPD stresses (perhaps somewhat disingenuously) that it is not about performance indicators or target-setting, but rather a tool for effectively managing what is, at 40,000 officers, the biggest police department in America. According to the department's own literature:

> 'Although statistics are the most visible part of the Compstat process they are not the most important part. The most important part of the Compstat process is leadership. It is leadership from the mayor and the police commissioner down to the patrol sergeant in the street which has made the department more effective than ever before. A critical focus for leadership . . . is the precinct commander. No element of the Compstat process has been more important than empowering precinct commanders, giving them authority to act and to innovate at their own discretion to fight crime' [Giuliani and Safir 1997].

Under Compstat, the NYPD also actively seeks out community opinion. Precinct commanders (lieutenants or captains), generally attend borough council meetings, and

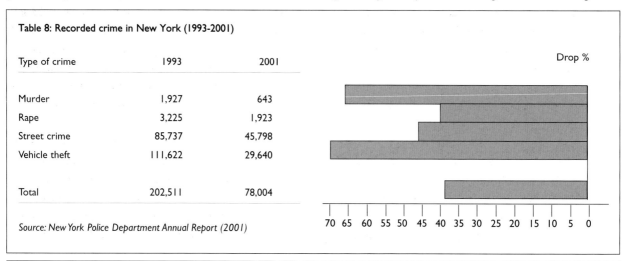

Table 8: Recorded crime in New York (1993-2001)

Type of crime	1993	2001
Murder	1,927	643
Rape	3,225	1,923
Street crime	85,737	45,798
Vehicle theft	111,622	29,640
Total	202,511	78,004

Source: New York Police Department Annual Report (2001)

send the information and opinions gleaned back to Compstat HQ. At Compstat meetings, therefore, the chief or commissioner can 'pull the file' on a borough council to see what is of concern and what the precinct commander has done about it. A 'Quality of Life Hotline' with a (freephone) 800 number allows members of the public to complain direct to police HQ. Conversely, Compstat feeds information back to the public, via a website detailing weekly crime figures by borough, precinct and district (see www.nyc.gov/html/nypd/html/pct/cspdf.html).

Compstat takes up a great deal of senior officer time. 'Pre meetings' held the day before the full weekly Compstat can take several hours and involve all senior operational chiefs of division. These are followed by an early morning meeting prior to Compstat to finalise details. The 'Comp' starts at 7am and lasts three hours, its timing being designed to minimize disruption to ordinary duties.

Compstat has had a dramatic impact on policing in New York. It has focused policing on efficient crime fighting rather than PR work and bureaucracy, forced patrol officers and detectives to work together, and increased communication between senior and junior ranks. The fall in New York's crime levels since Compstat's introduction has been startling (see Table 8). In 1993, New York was rated by the FBI as the United States' most dangerous city; by 2001, it was rated as the safest.

This dramatic success is not all to the credit of Compstat: police numbers in New York increased from 36,000 in 1993 to 40,000 in 2001. Also, other parts of America experienced similar falls in crime, reaffirming that crime trends have as much to with socio-economic changes as with policing. Between 1994 and 2000 arrests for violent crime fell 20% nationally, and even more steeply amongst juveniles and young adults, a trend partly attributable to the falling out of fashion of crack-cocaine [Butts and Travis 2002].

NYPD nonetheless continues to regard Compstat as an invaluable management tool, and variations of it have been adopted by many other American cities, including Chicago, Boston, Los Angeles, Baltimore and Newark. Though the potential for Compstat to be applied to the UK context can be debated, the central point is that it came about as a result of the accountability of local police forces to local political leaders.

Policing in Baltimore

The Baltimore City police department, with 3,300 officers, is one of the larger police departments in America. The Baltimore police commissioner is appointed by the mayor, who is directly elected. The mayor and commissioner work closely together and have very similar views on policing strategy.

The chief does not discuss current investigations with the mayor but the chief does see himself as a city employee. Like the fire chief, he is 'just another' chief officer. Police officers up to the rank of lieutenant have civil service employment rights, and for the most senior officers, a 6 year contract is usual. The contract does not overlap with the term of office of the mayor, so when there is a change of mayor there is no certainty that the the chief will serve out the rest of his contract [Interview, Deputy Commissioner McEntee, Baltimore PD HQ 2002].

All chief officers know that they serve at the pleasure of the Mayor. To balance their lack of job security, Baltimore has put in place a system of a one year buyout (or severance package) which is seen as a part of the salary benefit of the original contract. The Police Executive Research Forum (PERF) and the International Association of Chief Police Officers (IACP) in Washington act as 'headhunters' for police chiefs who are willing to move departments. So there are opportunities as well as risks for able chief officers.

The deputy commissioner of the Baltimore police explained that the department now relies on the Compstat system to manage police operations. The weekly meeting is rarely cancelled because it has 'to be seen as the big deal' by every officer. He had personally returned from holiday to attend, because the most senior officers 'need to be seen there'. Compstat provides data on crime for periods of 7 days, 28 days and one year for each police district in the city. The choice of which three districts will be reviewed at the next meeting is made by reference to the previous 28 day period. The two difficult areas in Baltimore are the western and eastern districts, where for the year to July there had already been 72 shootings and 49 murders. Although the statistic for the Western district represented a fifteen year low, these figures made Baltimore a more dangerous city than New York (by head of population).

For the Baltimore police department the real benefit of Compstat is that it has made the police 'go back to basics, which is crime'. Prior to Compstat, the orientation of policing in the city was towards attending 'community council meetings', or finding out how many police 'ride along' opportunities had been provided to the public. Meanwhile, 'there was all this crime that was not on the police agenda'. Since implementing Compstat, the police have made a big impact on crime, as resources have been targeted more accurately and patrol deployments are no longer random:

> 'Since 1999 even with a change in city administration and a change in police chief violent crime has come down 20%. This is a reflection of the success of the Compstat approach' [Interview, Deputy Commissioner McEntee, Baltimore PD 2002].

The Mayor of Baltimore is so impressed with Compstat that he has set up 'City Stat', an equivalent data tool which he uses to run other city services.

Conclusions from the United States

The locally driven and locally accountable system of policing in the US has a number of advantages. It fosters innovation, maintains active community involvement in setting policing agendas, allows for a flexible and responsive approach to police strategy, and avoids the worst excesses of a centralised and bureaucratic system.

Greater accountability

Given a suitable democratic framework, locally-led police forces are much more accountable to the communities they serve. The American model of local police management is reinforced by an historic commitment to public involvement in civic government. Local forces prioritise community contact, and police chiefs are clear that one of their core roles is to communicate with the community and respond to its needs [International Association of Chiefs of Police 1999].

> " Patrol builds public support, which itself encourages patrol. "

This was borne out by our field research. Police officers in Arlington stressed, for example, the close links made between the department and the community. The most important link was with civic associations, and 'every neighbourhood has a civic association or social group with which they can make contact'. In Philadelphia the police department has to deal not just with the mayor but also with regular town meetings, where complaints about policing can be made. 'What makes these meetings interesting is that they are usually televised, so complaints can be expected to be taken up with the police chief directly by the city mayor' [Interview, G. Wasserman, Philadelphia PD 2002]. Meanwhile, in New York City community councils have been set up for each police precinct, made up of 'upstanding members of the community'. While not seen as 'critics of the police' they provide a lot of 'good feedback' [Interview, J. Travis, Urban Institute, Washington DC 2002].

The emphasis on serving the local community translates into a strong commitment to the value of small policing departments. Research has shown that large departments are less efficient [Monkennen 1981; Nalla 1992]. They have a tendency to dilute uniform police presence as specialised units and bureaucracy proliferate. In bigger departments, fewer officers have immediate contact with the public [Loveday 1998]. In the words of one interviewee: 'In big departments it is usually the case that there are many people who are doing nothing. In Chicago, there were floors full of people doing nothing. Big agencies create the temptation of specialist teams while paperwork takes even more away from the job' [Interview, E. Lehrer, AEI Washington DC 2002].

According to the Heritage Foundation 'The size of the force has no effect on crime. The key question is, 'What do you do with the resources you have?' Local political control of the police encourages a strong commitment to active police patrols. Their use is seen in part as a commitment to accountability on the part of the police department. The effect reinforces itself. As Heritage argues:

'If the public have a positive perception of the police then the police will go out and patrol, because they are welcomed by the community. There is a strong morale issue here. Patrol activity builds public support which itself will actually encourage patrol activity' [Interview, E.R. Moffit, Heritage Foundation, Washington DC 2002].

Fostering innovation

The localised nature of policing in the US liberates police forces to develop policy as they see fit. The best innovate; the worst stagnate. National templates for good practice exist, but the real drivers of innovation are local police departments themselves - the true hot-houses of experimentation. As one interviewee put it:

'San Diego and Chicago Police Departments have both been innovative. The entrepreneurial spirit is encouraged, because they are allowed to run their own affairs.' [Interview, J. Travis, Urban Institute, Washington DC 2002].

At its heart, policing in the US is guided by a powerful democratic ethic. This encourages a form of policing that is responsive to local conditions, and to the wishes of local communities. Financial autonomy is key. Local police budgets can be adjusted by the mayor to finance new initiatives. And although the potential for national standardisation is limited, there is a degree of redistribution within cities and counties. In New York City, for example, 'what Wall Street pays Bedford Stuyvesant gets'.

As priorities change, so can police funding. In the 1990s New York faced a major homicide problem. Mayor Guiliani said that from 1989 to 1993 New York City experienced 'anywhere from 1,800 to 2,200 murders a year' [Guiliani 2002:71]. He responded by raising taxes to pay for another 4,000 police officers and police numbers grew further in his second term [Interview, J Travis, Urban Institute, Washington DC 2002]. Financial freedom gives local authorities the flexibility to make rapid changes to policing policies, funding and personnel.

Compstat is another example of the sort of local innovation that the US system encourages. As one commentator argued, Compstat is 'the most important development in public management in the US since World War Two' and it could never have evolved under a centralised system. 'It was a local development generated by a local problem and if police departments were centrally run then they could not have done what has been achieved in the NYPD.' [Interview, Heritage Foundation, Washington DC 2002]

There are other examples of local innovation. In Lowell, Massachusetts, the police chief largely abolished specialist units. Instead, he sent half the personnel from these units on 'street cop projects'. No-one was 'above' a patrol officer. The move was not popular with the police union, but they found it 'difficult to sustain their case, since the chief officer was out on patrol too'.

The approach succeeded. 'Police found that criminals in the main aren't smart. They are usually easy to locate and also to arrest. As the police department in Lowell has shown it's perfectly easy to identify and go and break up a crack house the same night, rather than to do what large departments do which is spend money and time subjecting the house to surveillance and the rest. In Lowell a crack house is hit the same day it's found, by a unit assembled in the shopping mall an hour before they move in' [Interview, E. Lehrer, AEI, Washington DC 2002].

Drawbacks of the US model

Local control inevitably translates into wide variations in performance. The degree to which local accountability can deliver effective policing depends on the vigour of local politics and the vigilance of local media. Where they are weak, corruption and incompetence can flourish.

The reliance on local taxes to fund policing is a key component of the US approach to policing. But it means that counties with high unemployment, low average incomes and a small tax base can become victims of a double whammy: high crime rates on the one hand, and inadequate resources to fund the necessary police response on the other.

But it seems clear that, for the USA as a whole, the gains from local control outweigh the costs. A nation of the civic-minded and politically engaged ensures that in most places, most of the time policing is truly owned and led by local communities. There is much in this model of policing for Britain to envy.

Notes

5   For extensive information on the US structure of policing, see http://faculty.ncwc.edu/toconnor/polstruct.htm.

6   These figures are not entirely consistent; due to rounding. Source: Justice Expenditure and Employment in the United States, 1999 (US Department of Justice, February 2002)

4. France

Policing in France

In the seventeenth century, France led the way in Europe in systematically nationalising policing. The legacy of that centralising approach is evident today. France now has three types of police force. The two biggest police forces are both national and have responsibility for rural and urban areas respectively. The Gendarmerie Nationale (GN) has responsibility for all rural areas and towns with a population of less than 10,000. The oldest police force in France, it is controlled by the Ministry of Defence and has a staff of 99,000. The Police Nationale (PN) is responsible for all urban areas and towns with a population of over 10,000. The PN is a civilian agency run from the Ministry of the Interior and has a staff of 130,000. It polices around 50% of the population but only around 5% of the territory of France. The third type of police force is the Municipal Police. It has grown rapidly since it was introduced in the 1980s, now employs 13,000 officers and is the responsibility of local Mayors.

The 'national' character of the PN is of relatively recent origin. Until 1941, the police in most French towns were financed and organised locally, providing service of variable quality. In 1900 the State had immediate control only of the forces of a few major cities. The extension of central state responsibility for policing in France was slow and there was considerable local opposition to the process of 'étatisation'. By 1920 the State had gained control of policing in Toulon and Nice, but failed in its attempt to take over the police force in Lille because of strong opposition. The turning point in the development of urban policing was the 1941 Vichy Government Law which made the state responsible for policing in all towns with a population of 10,000 or more [Horton 1995; Emsley 1987].

From 1941 on all police officers in the PN were recruited, paid and trained by the State. But no truly 'national' force was established until 1966 when the privileged status of the Prefecture of Paris was removed, and the Paris police were finally integrated into the PN.

Rising crime

Since 1998 France has experienced rapidly increasing levels of recorded crime. In 2001, crime rose 8%, making it a core election issue in the 2002 Presidential election [*International Herald Tribune*, 3/4/02]. International comparisons are no more encouraging, with France in the bottom fifteen countries worldwide for both serious assault and theft. [Interpol 1999]. France has been poor about publishing crime statistics, perhaps again a feature of a centralised, bureaucratic state with little local accountability for policing. Perhaps due to the poor rapport between police and public, crime reporting rates are even lower than in other European states. Low reporting levels and limited transparency have blocked public debate on crime and policing, and fostered the far right, whose willingness to discuss crime and policing (though often in inflammatory and racist terms), wins public support.

In the late 1990s, crime was the third biggest political issue in France. Street crime was one key worry: 20% of French citizens felt unsafe walking in their area after dark. And the former chief superintendent of the Renseignements Generaux, the government's police intelligence agency, has alleged that the government recategorised public disorder in order to finesse violent disorder statistics [*International Herald Tribune*, 3/4/02].

Effects of centralisation

The French experience offers a valuable case study of the costs and benefits of eliminating local police forces, and replacing them with a centrally administered state service. Since its introduction, the centralised PN (and to a lesser extent the GN) has developed various dysfunctional characteristics, causing increasing concern to successive French governments.

In the larger cities the PN had by the 1980s 'practically abandoned the investigation of theft and break-ins' [R Levy *et al* 2002]. Since these offences constitute the highest volume crimes in most urban areas, this development amounted to a significant reduction in policing service.

In addition to such operational compromises, there is evidence of organisational failures in the PN. These include:

- waste and inflexibility resulting from a centralised system of budgetary management [Horton 1995:114];
- requirement that 80% of administrative posts in central directorates responsible for finance, communications and personnel are filled by police officers [Horton ibid];
- permanent assignments of police officers to specific duties unrelated to crime-fighting (e.g. as chauffeurs or car mechanics) [Horton ibid] ;
- inflexible shift systems negotiated by national police unions reducing the amount of officer time available for patrol work. (Five-day cycles of duty concentrated into two and half days, leaving officers free to supplement their income by undeclared work outside their police duties) [Horton 1995:127 and 128];
- abuse of sick leave leading to high rates of absenteeism [Horton 1995:128];
- insistence on minimum of two to three officers per foot patrol/police vehicle [Horton 1995:129];
- use of police auxiliaries to supplement beat patrol work [Horton 1995:125]; and
- bureaucratic crime recording systems which discourage reporting of incidents by the public [Levy et al 2002:6].

Reforms from the 1980s onwards

Until the 1980s the main political priority for the French police was to defend the State against riots and other threats to public order. After these threats receded, the administration of both the PN and GN was reviewed.

The first reform that resulted was the partial devolution of responsibility for finance from the centre to the localities. Before the reform local branches of the PN and GN needed to apply to Paris if they wanted to purchase items such as lamps and typewriters, or wanted to move police vehicles from one policing area to another. Following reform in 1989 local Prefects began to share responsibility for the 'local' police budget with the Ministry of the Interior. However, the devolution of control over budgets did not extend to salaries or capital spending, despite the fact that there was 'general enthusiasm among senior police officers about the possibility of gaining responsibility for personnel management' [Horton 1995:116].

In the 1980s the PN adopted a national strategy of 'police de proximité', or neighbourhood policing. This was encouraged by central government, which thought that lessons could be learned from community policing experience in England [Horton 1995]. It involved particular police officers patrolling a defined territory on a regular basis and making systematic contact with the local population. One of its central objectives was to improve police-public relations, and the intention was that it would link up with local crime prevention initiatives pursued by Mayors through their municipal police forces (see below).

This attempt to adapt centrally-run policing to local needs has not been a complete success. 'Despite all the ministerial exhortation on the subject of neighbourhood policing, the spread of this policing technique has been patchy, and the type of policing provided in its name has varied considerably from one place to another' [Horton 1995:141]. There has been resistance from PN officers who do not see preventative policing as 'real police work', and for whom crime investigation comes first. Despite a 'massive training effort to instil the new doctrine into the PN, official audits show that beat officers do not adhere to this policy' [Levy et al 2002:7]. Officers have little incentive to integrate their activities with 'Local Safety Plans', since local chiefs of police are accountable only to the central authorities and their local representative the Prefect. Elected Mayors have no influence over the PN.

Local policing is further undermined by the GN and PN's recruitment policy, under which officers are assigned to any department in France, and 'it is thought preferable not to send an officer to the region he comes from, because loyalty to the central authorities should take precedence over an officer's loyalty to his place of origin and the community to which he belongs.' As a result of this deliberate policy, 'urban police departments have become detachments of the state police with very few social and functional ties with the community they serve' [Levy et al 2002:7].

The growth of municipal police forces

Many French mayors were not willing to wait for national reforms of the PN and GN to reverse the fall in the provision of uniform patrol activity. In the 1980s they began to explore ways of exploiting the Loi Municipale of 1884 [Journes 1993] which gives mayors responsibility for public order within their communes and the power to appoint all municipal employees including municipal police constables and inspectors. No doubt there were other factors which contributed towards the growth of municipal police forces: for right wing councils it may have reflected a suspicion of the then Socialist government [Horton 1995:71]; and some Mayors probably sought the prestige of commanding their own police force. But Horton notes that 'For many communes, including those on the Left, the main motivation was the strong desire to respond to public demand for more uniformed officers on the street - a demand which was not being met by the services of the PN and the GN' [Horton 1995:71].

The result was rapid growth in the number of municipal police forces. Between 1984 and 1993 their number rose from 1,748 to 2,860, with a corresponding increase in personnel from 5,641 to 10,000. The last 15 years have seen further expansion of municipal forces, so that in 2002 there are approximately 3,000 of them employing a total staff of 13,000.

Many of the municipal forces employ only a small number of police officers. Only 600 have five or more municipal constables, while only ten have more than 100 officers [R Levy et al 2002]. The nature of their role and function also varies. In some areas officers are employed on a general patrol basis but elsewhere in the bigger cities they work on a 24-hour shift basis. In some areas like Nice and Cannes, the police are armed; in many others they are not. In general, pay rates are lower than for the PN and training is also very limited. This reflects the fact that their role is largely to provide public reassurance and not to investigate crimes.

The official view is that the municipal police are complementary to the PN and GN, and not a challenge to them. They are not engaged in fighting crime; their role is to enforce municipal regulations, to help prevent crime through visible patrol and, in part, to relieve the PN of menial tasks like traffic control. While they have a power of arrest they do not possess any investigative powers; on an arrest, the municipal police pass the case on to the PN or GN. It is difficult to gauge what impact the municipal police forces have had on local crime rates - not least because no record is kept by municipalities of crimes recorded in their areas [Interview, R. Levy 2002].

French police unions have been hostile to the development of municipal police, and in particular to the lack of visible distinction between them and the PN and GN. This may explain the decision of the last Socialist government to limit the right of the municipal police to carry weapons, and to require that their uniforms clearly distinguish them from the PN and GN.

Conclusions

In France, there is little concept of the need for police forces to be directly accountable to elected politicians. There are no equivalents to the UK's police authorities. The national parliament, the Assemblée Nationale, does not check up on how the executive uses its powers over the police, and locally elected officials have no power over the PN or GN.

Municipal police forces do report to locally elected mayors and are financed out of municipal taxes. All agents including the chief are municipal officers under the control of the mayor. But even this measure of local democratic accountability has been eroded by central government's decision to require all municipalities with five or more officers to establish a contract with the local prefect. This contract establishes where and when municipal officers can intervene, and how that intervention will be coordinated with either the PN or the GN [Levy 2002].

To the extent that there is any commitment in France to a local model of policing, it is best understood as a matter of operational tactics, rather than political structure. While it is true that the government is encouraging the PN and GN to participate in 'Local Safety Plans', and is prepared to grant some discretion over operations to local police forces, there is no sign of the central State relinquishing control over either force.

Some students of the French approach to policing argue that centralisation offers advantages:

- standardised information technology provision creates better communication between regions;
- good practice in policing in one area can be quickly disseminated to all areas in France; and
- there are aspects of policing which it may make sense to provide nationally e.g. policing of motorway traffic [Horton 1995:163].

But it also appears that central control can undermine the fight against crime because it:

- engenders a police culture that is resistant to local crime prevention initiatives; and
- entrenches a system of national bargaining on pay and conditions which make it hard to reverse the fall in visible police patrol [Loveday 1999].

The clearest evidence that central police services in France have failed to deliver what the public wants is provided by the rapid proliferation of municipal police forces in the last 20 years. It is a sign of the deep-rooted ness of France's 'dirigiste' approach that central government's response has been to begin to bring these forces under the same central control as the PN and the GN, and to limit the powers of the locally elected mayors who set them up.

5. The Netherlands

Policing in the Netherlands

There are 45,000 people employed in the police service in the Netherlands, of whom 35,000 are uniformed and CID officers, and 10,000 are administrative and other civilian staff. Until 1993, the country had 148 police forces which followed the boundaries of the different municipalities. There were two types of force. Larger municipalities had a 'city police' force (Gemeentepolitie), whereas rural areas had a 'state police' force (Rijkspolitie).

The Police Act of 1993 ended the fragmentation of the Dutch police and brought in a new system of 25 regional forces, ranging in size from 500-5,000 officers. Although municipalities have the discretion to hire more police for their local force, only 1-2% of police funding is provided on a local basis. The rest is controlled by the Minister of Home Affairs and Kingdom Relations.

In addition to the regional forces, there is a National Police Agency (KLPD) which employs 3,500 people. The KLPD supports regional police forces with its specialist detective squads, and is responsible for national police functions like royal and diplomatic protection. It also incorporates the railways and waterways police.

The management of regional police forces is the responsibility of what is known as the 'Triangle'. This comprises the mayor of the largest municipality in the police region, the public prosecutor for the judicial region (which has different borders from both the police region and the municipalities) and the chief of police. The mayor is appointed by the Minister of Home Affairs, and is responsible for maintaining public order. The public prosecutor is appointed by the Minister of Justice, and is responsible for prosecuting criminal offences.

A populist backlash against rising crime

Over the last year, policing has been at the heart of some dramatic developments in Dutch politics. Violent crime in 2001 was 11% higher than in 2000 and 35% higher than in 1997 [Statistics Netherlands Press Release, 27/09/02], triggering a popular backlash. The perception that in the major cities a lot of violent crime was linked to ethnic minorities led to the rapid rise of the extreme-right List Pym Fortuyn (LPF). The party won 35% of the vote in local elections in Rotterdam in March 2001, and gained 26 out of 150 seats in Parliament in the national elections held in the immediate aftermath of Pym Fortuyn's murder in May 2002.

LPF members in Rotterdam claimed that they suffered from 'the worst police force in the most violent city in the Netherlands', and attributed their electoral success to the fact that they alone amongst political parties addressed the problem. They complained that 'in Rotterdam the police don't focus on results and show no interest in public opinion on crime in the city. They go for easy options such as car-parking, but not crime.' [Interview, LPF members, Rotterdam City Hall 2000]

Similar observations were made in Amsterdam. There have been growing complaints about the existence of no-go areas in the south of the city. This has led to calls for the police to 'make clear who's boss in public spaces'. Both mayor and police seem to have recognised the threat of vigilantism if no action is taken against prostitution and drug dealing [Interview, M.J. Bezuyen, Stadhuis Amstel, Amsterdam 2002]. In the aftermath of the strong LPF showing in the 2002 elections, both mainstream political parties (the Liberals and Christian Democrats) have adopted more proactive policies on 'security' (read crime) in the run-up to elections in January 2003 [*The Economist*, 30/11/02].

Policing strategies

The perceived failure of policing in Dutch inner cities has its roots in the twenty-year dominance of a centrally imposed community policing strategy. In 1977 there was a Report on Police Organisational Structures (POS report) which led to a reorganisation of the police in the 1980s. The POS report argued that 'effectiveness... requires that the police service should be provided by geographically decentralised, comparatively small units that become associated with social groupings in the city or region and that will be responsible for providing overall policing in their territory'. The Report suggested that this new approach should replace the 'law enforcement role', which had hitherto received excessive emphasis and resulted in a distancing of the police from the community.

> " " The police are your best friend " "

The local team model of policing which was implemented in the 1980s had strong parallels with the community policing approach developed in Britain. Its objective was to bring 'the police closer to the people they serve, improving cooperation with other agencies and developing a planned approach to police work' [Jones 1995:96]. But in the Netherlands, the community policing model went much further. The POS report also saw a role for the police in the 'democratisation of society', and argued that 'the ultimate purpose of government and hence of the police is to create the conditions for the promotion of the essential features of democracy such as personal, political, social and economic freedom, equality and social justice' [Jones 1995:97]. The new approach was reflected in the slogan that was used to promote the police in the 1980s: 'The police are your best friend.'

The Dutch community policing strategy became a 'professional ideology' which was taught in the Police Academy to the people who are now the country's senior police officers. It led directly to the liberal approach to drug use and prostitution for which the Netherlands has become famous. Dutch police argue that tolerating the sale of small amounts of soft drugs in Dutch cities 'allows them to concentrate on more serious drugs offences' [Jones 1995:48]. The operation of sex clubs and brothels is also tolerated as part of a strategy of containment rather than elimination [Jones 1995:97].

Reflecting the view that the main purpose of the police was no longer to fight crime but to identify and diffuse social conflicts before they became serious, the police in Amsterdam set up 'special neighbourhood offices' designed to deal with broader social problems in their areas [Interview, M.J. Bezuyen, Stadhuis Amstel, Amsterdam 2002].

The community policing strategy has recently attracted increasing criticism, and not just from supporters of the LPF. A senior Dutch politician described it as 'extreme' and expressed frustration with the emphasis placed on 'accommodating tensions' and 'avoiding a confrontational approach' with ethnic minorities; as a result, police officers were simply not equipped to deal with violent drug-related crime [Interview, Senator Uriel Rosenthal, Volkspartij voor Vrijheid en Democratie, Rotterdam 2002]. Opposition to community policing has become particularly vocal in inner cities where the level of victimisation has been consistently higher than elsewhere [Interview, M. de la Torre, The Hague, 2002]; in such areas pressure is growing for the police to focus on fighting crime and give up their role as unofficial social workers.

Police accountability

In the Netherlands, inner city residents unhappy with the standard of policing have difficulty in communicating their concerns and influencing police priorities. LPF members in Rotterdam complained that police officers 'appear to be focused on the police chief and the hierarchy rather than the public interest'. As a crown appointment, the police chief is not accountable to the community he serves and 'can't be fired.' Chiefs of police spend much of 'their time politicking with the mayor and the prosecutor' [Interview, Politie, The Hague 2002] rather than finding out what is really happening on the streets. 'They think they're on top of things but often they don't know more than 10% of what's really going on. If you want to know how bad things are in urban areas you need to go to the housing corporations, not the police' [Interview, U. Rosenthal, Rotterdam 2002].

Professor Muller has noted that 'police forces seldom give a detailed account to the mayor of the way they conduct their policies. Town councils generally approve reports by the police without much discussion. When it comes to the management of the police, democratic accountability is essentially non-existent' [Muller 2003:8].

One obvious way for the public to hold the police to account would be through the mayor. But Dutch mayors are also Crown appointees, and until now little in their nomination or appointment process has made it likely that they would be responsive to the wishes of the local community.

The process of nominating candidates for mayor has just been reformed. Previously, the appointment resulted from a secretive nomination process, involving backroom deals by the main political parties. Mayors did not even have to come from the city to which they were appointed. For this reason, they were very unlikely to have an instinctive feel for what local people wanted.

Legislation passed in 2001 gives city councils (whose members are elected), the right to present a 'recommended candidate' to the Minister. While this should improve the chances of a mayor being in touch with the concerns of the local community, he is always likely to put greater store by the ministerial authority that appointed him, rather than the locally elected one that nominated him. And although mayors are technically accountable to the elected councils, and can be removed if they lose a vote of no confidence, the use of this mechanism is 'highly unusual' [Interview, M.J. Bezuyen, Amsterdam 2002].

There has been some debate about the introduction of directly elected mayors. The LPF in Rotterdam would like to be able to make their police chief accountable by having him report to an elected mayor who they can 'get rid of'. The Dutch Liberal Party has visited New York to learn from the success of Mayor Giuliani, and there is now a growing body of support for mayoral elections to replace crown appointments. 'If there were directly elected mayors there would probably be no support for the community policing strategy pursued by all police forces.' [Interview, U. Rosenthal, Rotterdam 2002].

> " Public bodies should not always do what the public think they should do "

But there remains resistance to the idea - most of it based on the paternalist idea that the people do not always know best. 'Public bodies should not always do what the public think they should do' [Interview, M.J. Bezuyen, Mayor's Office Amsterdam 2002]. Some expressed the concern that the dominance of the mayor in relation to the police could pose a problem if he were elected, as there was a need for 'rational decision-making'. Others have noted that the introduction of elected mayors would require a fundamental reorganisation of local government and that there is little support for this [Interview, E. Muller, The Hague 2002].

Tension between regionalisation and democratic accountability

Although elected mayors would provide a more direct channel for public pressure on the police, the regional structure of the police service would still give each police chief multiple reporting lines, making accountability imperfect. Each chief of police is currently responsible for a region covering a number of different municipalities, so he has to balance the concerns of a number of different mayors. This has created tensions. Smaller towns and villages complain that 'larger cities take priority in the allocation of police resources at their expense' [Interview, Politie, The Hague 2002]. The mayors within each region only meet a few times a year to consider policing issues. [Interview, M.J. Bezuyen, Amsterdam 2002].

Elected mayors' ability to direct police chiefs to change their approach to policing in their city in response to public demand would therefore be limited under the regional system. Regional police chiefs will always be able to play off one mayor against another, whether they are elected or not. The only way that clear democratic accountability could be achieved within the Dutch regional system would be if police chiefs reported to an elected official who represented an area with the same boundaries as that for which the police chief was responsible. In a country where the boundaries of the police regions, the municipalities, the provinces and the judicial regions are all different, this is a distant prospect.

Some Dutch commentators believe that anomalies of this kind show that more centralisation is required, and that the creation of regional forces is just the first stage in a process that will lead to a national force under a single Minister for the Police, whose accountability derives from general elections to the Dutch parliament.

Professor Muller argues that 'there is a need for a formal external and independent civilian structure to control the police' and concludes that as elected municipal councils do not demonstrate much interest in bringing the police to account there is a vacuum which needs to be filled by a national body in which the 'government has primacy' [Muller 2003:6].

Conclusions

The lack of police accountability to the public in the Netherlands has created a pressure cooker of public discontent, especially in the major cities. The police are seen as divorced from the communities they serve, and obsessed with an out-of-date and politically-correct strategy which fails to deal with the growing problem of urban crime. There is support for introducing a greater measure of democratic accountability by electing mayors, who are currently appointed. On its own, however, such a reform would be unlikely to produce dramatic improvements in police accountability, since regional police forces serve many different communities and mayors.

6. Findings and recommendations

Research findings

Central control does not deliver more effective policing

There is little evidence that the centralised approaches to policing adopted in the UK, France and Netherlands have delivered improvements in fighting crime or providing public reassurance.

- In the UK, successive police reform Acts have tightened Home Office control over local police forces. But there is little evidence that central imposition of performance targets and initiatives has improved policing.
- In France, the two national police forces (Police and Gendarmerie Nationale) appear to be victims of bureaucratic inertia. Though pressure from local communities for more visible policing has prompted many mayors to set up their own municipal forces, central government is now trying to bring these back under its own control. Central government has responded to public anxiety over crime - expressed in the huge rise in the far-right vote in 2002's presidential election - with a strategy of neighbourhood policing ('police de proximité'). But there is no evidence that this has stopped the French police from looking to Paris for instructions, rather than to the communities they serve.
- In the Netherlands, urban police forces' failure to fight crime was one of the main reasons why so many people in the large cities voted for the anti-immigrant party List Pym Fortuyn. Public frustration is a result of the lack of accountability of centrally-appointed Dutch police chiefs, who pursue their own agendas rather than those of the communities they serve.

Local control makes policing more responsive, innovative, efficient and accountable

The US experience shows that police forces which operate under the control of locally elected officials are more responsive to local demands, more innovative in developing new policing strategies, and deliver a higher level of uniformed presence on the streets. In major American cities such as New York and Baltimore a renewed emphasis on targeting crime, and the assumption of responsibility by the police for 'quality of life' issues, have been both popular and effective. Although the fall in crime rates across the US has been assisted by a number of underlying demographic and social trends, changes in policing in response to community pressures and strong mayoral leadership have also made a major contribution.

A key element of local control of policing in the US is local financing. Although federal funds are made available to encourage forces to undertake specific programmes, the vast bulk of funding for US forces is raised from local taxes set by the Mayor and Council or the county board.

The control of policing by local politicians clearly creates opportunities for corruption and politically motivated policing. It is clear that locally controlled police forces are unlikely vigorously to prosecute the misdemeanours of their political masters. There have been several such scandals in the US, both in large cities such as Los Angeles and Chicago, and in smaller ones such as Providence, Rhode Island and Camden, New Jersey. The most effective protection against corruption is provided by a combination of well-financed and genuinely independent local audit bodies, fearless and vigorous local media, and a strong national police agency with the power and resources to bring corrupt local officials to book.

Constabulary independence insulates the police from local community pressures

In Britain, the convention of constabulary independence has been used by the police as a shield against pressure from local communities and politicians. Police officers in the US have no equivalent barriers to hide behind, and although junior ranks benefit from basic civil service employment rights, police chiefs and commissioners serve 'at the pleasure of the mayor or county board' on short-term contracts. As a result US police forces are much more responsive to the demands of the public they serve.

Police forces with multiple reporting lines function less well than those with single reporting lines

Attempts to minimise any one individual's influence over policing by sharing control of the police among a number of different officials or bodies tend to confuse the public, place conflicting demands on the police and create opportunities for irresponsible police chiefs to evade responsibility for their performance.

- In the UK, police authorities comprising local councillors, magistrates and independent members nominated by the Home Office have achieved almost no public profile, and are seen as powerless ciphers.
- In France, the requirement that each municipal force report to central government's representative, the Prefect, as well as to the local mayor has muddled

policing priorities, and undermined the original purpose of the municipal forces, which was to respond to public demands.

- In the Netherlands, the 'Triangle' system whereby each police chief reports both to the mayor of the largest municipality in the region and the public prosecutor has made it possible for police to pursue their own professional ideology and ignore rising frustration among inner city residents.
- In the US, police forces which are clearly under the control of the Mayor (as in New York) have been more successful in fighting crime and gaining public confidence, and less prone to corruption and other scandal, than police forces whose accountability is divided between a Board of Commissioners, the Council and the Mayor (as in Los Angeles).

Top down performance measurement distorts police priorities and wastes officer time; bottom up performance measurement is a useful management tool which helps police forces become more effective.

The central imposition of performance indicators and targets as practised in the UK can impede good policing and diminishes local accountability:

- Performance data are published long after the end of the reporting periods to which they relate. As a result they are of little use in planning day-to-day operations.
- The singling out by central government of specific targets distorts police priorities, impedes intelligent planning of operations and demotivates professional managers.

The introduction of Compstat, in contrast, has greatly assisted police force management in several cities in the US:

- Performance data are published within a week of collection, enabling swift responses to operational shortfalls and changes in criminal activity on the ground.
- Precinct commanders are not measured against arbitrary targets imposed from above, but against their peers, against their prior performance and against the expectations of the communities they serve.

Compstat contributes to public confidence in the police since data are made publicly available online within two weeks of collection, and lines of responsibility for success or failure are clear.

There is no evidence that large forces are more effective than small forces at fighting crime and providing public reassurance.

Growing doubts about police force amalgamations are justified. Larger police forces are more likely to divert resources into the creation of specialist teams, and as a result appear to have greater difficulty in sustaining visible policing than smaller forces.

- In the UK, amalgamated forces such as West Mercia and Thames Valley perform worse than traditional county forces responsible for areas with comparable socioeconomic characteristics. The best performing forces in the UK are small forces such as Gwent and Suffolk.
- The amalgamation of forces in the Netherlands has created tension and confused reporting lines, as each area now covers several different mayors and prosecutors.
- In the US there is no commitment to a standard or optimum size of police department. The size of any police force is determined by the boundaries of the community which it serves, and which pays for it through local taxation.

There is a role for a national police force with specialist capabilities

There are some policing functions which do not naturally confine themselves to a particular area of the country e.g.

government, diplomatic and royal protection. The campaign against terrorism is another area best dealt with nationally. There are also some crimes which are rare, serious and highly complex e.g. fraud, international drug-smuggling and organised crime. It is unrealistic to expect each local police force to have the specialist skills to investigate such offences effectively. The best solution is to have a national police agency which fulfils national policing functions and supports local police forces as needed e.g. the FBI in the US and the KLPD in the Netherlands.

Principles of governance

From the findings set out in this report we have derived a number of principles for the good governance of policing:

Local police forces should be accountable to local communities

Police forces responsible for maintaining public order and fighting crime in a defined local community should report to and be overseen by an authority that is elected by that community. This authority should set the targets, priorities and budgets that it feels are appropriate. It should have the power to replace a chief officer if it believes that the force is failing to deliver results.

A key implication of local control is that central government should not impose bureaucratic systems of performance measurement on local forces. Forces should be free to develop information systems which best assist their own internal management, and which meet the demands of local elected authorities for performance disclosure.

Constabulary independence should be strictly limited

The convention of constabulary independence should be more tightly defined. While the locally-elected authority overseeing the police should not have the right to intervene in specific criminal cases or to hire and fire anyone but the most senior officers, there should be no limit on its ability to determine the strategy, priorities and budget of the force, or subject its operations to scrutiny.

Accountability should be focused and not diffuse

Accountability is best achieved by having a single elected individual act on behalf of the public. This creates a focus for public attention and police reporting. The elected overseer should be at liberty to appoint people with relevant expertise or complementary perspectives to a board of advisors.

Local people should pay for policing through local taxes

If local police forces are to be genuinely accountable to the communities they serve, most of the money that pays for them must be raised from local taxes. These taxes should not only be raised locally, but set by the local authorities to whom the forces report. Only forces covering poor areas with small tax-bases should receive substantial central government grant.

Police forces under local political control should be closely inspected for evidence of corruption

A necessary counterpart of local control for police forces is a tough anti-corruption regime involving regular audits by an apolitical body which can pass cases of suspected wrongdoing to a national police agency for investigation and prosecution.

Police force boundaries should match natural community boundaries

The boundaries of the area served by each police force should coincide with the natural boundaries of a distinct community and, as far as possible, the boundaries of other administrative and political authorities responsible for providing services to that community. This will assist the coordination of policing with the other authorities that have an impact on public order and quality of life. For this reason, there should be no drive for uniformity in the size of police forces. In some parts of the country, it may make most sense to have a county force and in others a district or town force.

Specialist police functions should be brought together in a single national force

Specialist police functions with national scope (currently largely performed by the Met's Scotland Yard), should be located in a national police agency that reports to central government. Local forces should be encouraged to call on the expertise of these specialist teams as and when local chief officers determine.

Policy Options for Local Accountability

Police forces should be accountable to elected representatives of the local community. The key ingredients of accountability are the power to appoint and dismiss senior police officers such as the chief constable (and possibly his or her deputies), as well as the power to set a force's priorities and determine its budget. Making police forces in the UK locally accountable could be achieved in a number of different ways. Before making final recommendations, let us review the pros and cons of the main alternatives:

Directly elected police authorities

One approach would be to take existing police authorities and introduce local direct elections for all (or a majority of) their members.

The advantages of this approach are that it would:
- entail the least amount of reorganization as it would be based on existing police authority/force arrangements;
- give police authorities a visibility and legitimacy they currently lack;
- give local people with a particular interest in or experience of policing an opportunity to represent their local community without standing for election.

The disadvantages of this approach are that:
- authority and accountability would be shared between several individuals, none of whom would be likely to attract a very high profile;

- confronted by a new group of locally elected officials in addition to local councillors, the public might be confused about their respective responsibilities;
- it might encourage turf battles between elected police authority members and local councillors responsible for other services contributing to public safety and crime prevention;
- if all police authority members were elected, the public would forfeit the services of useful independent members.

Directly elected policy authority chairman or 'sheriff'

Another approach would for the chairman of the police authority to be directly elected by the local community. He or she could then be supported by a panel of appointees, possibly including local councillors and experts nominated by HMIC. The key power to hire and fire senior police officers would rest with the elected chairman.

The advantages of this approach are that it would:

- create a role with high visibility and a clear focus for local accountability;
- be based on existing police authority/force structures.

The main disadvantage of this approach is that:

- it could lead to rivalry between council leaders and elected chairmen of police authorities, impeding coordinated action against crime.

Police forces to be accountable to elected mayors and council leaders

An alternative approach would be to give responsibility for police oversight to existing local leaders, specifically elected mayors where they exist and, elsewhere, the leaders of district, council or unitary authorities. The police authority could then be reconstituted as an advisory panel combining both local councillors (or assembly members) and expert appointees.

The advantages of this approach are that:

- mayors and council leaders would be well placed to ensure coordination between local authority and police

priorities, boosting existing 'community safety partnerships';

- the public (and media) would have a single focus for their concerns about local quality of life, encouraging higher turnouts in local elections;
- duplication of effort would be avoided.

The disadvantages of this approach are that:

- some police forces cover a number of different local authority areas, and would therefore have to be broken up so as to coincide with local authority boundaries;
- most local authority leaders are indirectly elected and therefore have a lower public profile and less legitimacy than a directly elected police authority chairman.

Recommendations

We propose the following reforms to policing in England and Wales because we believe that they will:

- increase police forces' responsiveness to the concerns of the communities they serve;
- increase public confidence in the police;
- encourage innovation and diversity in the management of policing.

We recommend that:

Police should be made directly accountable to mayors and council leaders

Where existing police force boundaries are identical to those of an elected Mayor or unitary authority, the chief constable should report to the Mayor or the leader of the unitary authority.

In counties where there are both country and district councils, there should be referenda to determine whether people feel stronger associations with their district or their county. People should be offered the choice of being policed by district forces reporting to the leaders of the district councils, or by a county force reporting to the leader of the county council.

In areas with amalgamated forces covering more than one county (e.g. Devon and Cornwall), the force should be split up into county or district forces as decided in local referenda (as above).

Where the boundaries of a police basic command unit (BCU) do not coincide with the boundaries of a local authority district, the BCU boundaries should be adjusted accordingly.

Mayors and council leaders should be subject to overview and scrutiny by a police committee and require approval by elected assemblies and councils for the policing budget and strategy

Each council leader and mayor taking responsibility for the police should be required to submit the policing budget for approval by the full council or assembly as part of the normal budgeting process. They should also be required to set up an overview and scrutiny committee to review their executive decisions on policing and provision should be made for the appointment of lay members to sit alongside elected councillors/assembly members on these committees.

Police chief constables should be put on short term contracts

Police chief constables and assistant chief constables should be employed on short-term contracts as in the United States. It should be possible for the mayor or council leader to dismiss a chief constable or an assistant chief constable with compensation determined according to a pre-agreed severance provision in the contract.

The convention of constabulary independence should be limited

Parliament should define in statute the convention of constabulary independence, so as to make it clear that direction of strategy and operational priorities by a mayor or council leader is permissible, though intervention in individual operations or arrests is not.

Police forces should be locally financed

Most of the cost of each local police force should be funded out of local taxation. The taxes used to raise these funds should be determined and raised by the institution whose leader oversees the force. A county force should be funded by county taxes raised by the county council. A district force should be funded by district taxes raised by the district council.

In deprived areas of the country there will be need for continuing central government grant to fund policing. However, even in these areas a substantial proportion of the costs of policing should be financed out of local taxation.

The reform of police funding is likely to be part of a wider transfer of financial responsibility and tax-raising powers from central to local government. How this should work is a separate question which will the subject of future research by Policy Exchagne.

HMIC should focus on audits and investigating possible corruption

HMIC should be redirected towards a strict audit function, and be given a clear mandate and adequate resources to scrutinise all forces for any evidence of corruption, discrimination or political bias. Local councils and assemblies responsible for overseeing police forces should be required to publicise HMIC reports widely.

National Crime Agency should be established for national policing priorities and specialist operations

Police functions with a national or international dimension (e.g. counter-terrorism, royal and government protection), should be transferred from the Metropolitan Police to a National Crime Agency, whose chief officer should report to the Home Secretary. The agency should incorporate the existing National Crime Squad and National Criminal Intelligence Service.

The National Crime Agency should develop specialist teams focusing on particular types of crime or methods of detection. Local forces should be encouraged to call on the National Crime Agency for assistance when they need specialist support.

The National Crime Agency should work closely with HMIC in its anti-corruption function and be responsible for investigating and bringing forward for prosecution any offences committed by local police forces, mayors or members of local authorities.

National Police Holding Body should be set up to handle residual assets

Assets currently belonging to individual police forces which are not integral to individual forces' local functions (e.g. police training colleges, forensic laboratories etc) should be transferred to a National Police Holding Body administered by a board appointed by the Home Office. Within five years, the National Police Holding Body should dispose of all assets by selling them to local authorities, floating them off as self-financing stand-alone institutions or shutting them down. Experience of residuary bodies from the 1980s suggests that this could be accomplished with relative ease.

Appendix A: Local Voices, Local Choices ICM Poll 24–25 April 2002

In April 2002 ICM Research Limited carried out an opinion poll for Policy Exchange, looking at attitudes towards local services and their accountability. In the context of police accountability, these results are very interesting.

- Two-thirds (68 percent) of the British population believe they have little or no impact on setting priorities for local public services. Across different social classes, age groups and British regions, a majority feel they have little or no influence in setting local service priorities.

- The public are evenly split between those who think that the people who currently run local public services are accountable for their decisions and performance - and those who think that they are not.

- An overwhelming 80 percent of respondents would like

to have more input into the priorities set for local public services (with only 17 percent disagreeing).

- More local input into local services would make half of the population (48 percent) more likely to vote in local elections. While this isn't dramatic, broken down by age, 25-34 year-olds would be 64 percent more likely to vote. Given existing voting patterns, this would be a significant side-benefit.

- Just over half (58 percent) of those polled believe that locally elected management of public services would provide a better service (just seven percent think it would lead to poorer services). Incidentally, the over-65s are most bleak about the benefits of local control here - with 31 percent, against 20 percent for other age groups, thinking it would stay the same.

Q1: How much input do you believe you currently have into the priorities set for your local public services – i.e. schools, hospitals and the police?

	Total	Sex		Age						Social Class				Region				
		Male	Fe-male	18-24	25-34	35-44	45-54	55-64	65+	AB	C1	C2	DE	South East	Mid-lands	North Eng-land	Wales & South West	Scot-land
Unweighted base	1000	470	530	90	183	208	181	135	203	302	267	206	225	270	246	252	142	90
Weighted base	1000	486	514	109	195	190	170	131	204	232	274	218	276	266	258	250	137	89
A great deal of input (4)	61 6%	32 6%	29 6%	4 4%	8 4%	12 6%	8 5%	9 7%	20 10%	7 3%	19 7%	14 6%	21 8%	16 6%	16 6%	19 8%	3 2%	7 8%
Some input (3)	230 23%	83 17%	146 28%	22 20%	41 21%	43 23%	38 22%	30 23%	57 28%	49 21%	56 20%	50 23%	74 27%	59 22%	48 19%	67 27%	35 26%	20 22%
Little input (2)	378 38%	194 40%	183 36%	47 43%	86 44%	73 38%	63 37%	49 37%	60 29%	95 41%	100 37%	91 42%	91 33%	92 34%	107 42%	88 35%	51 37%	40 45%
No input at all (1)	304 30%	167 34%	137 27%	33 30%	57 29%	60 32%	58 34%	39 30%	57 28%	77 33%	94 34%	58 27%	74 27%	91 34%	83 32%	70 28%	41 30%	20 22%
Don't know	28 3%	9 2%	18 4%	3 3%	4 2%	2 1%	3 2%	5 4%	10 5%	3 1%	4 2%	5 2%	16 6%	8 3%	3 1%	6 2%	8 6%	3 3%
Mean	2.05	1.96	2.14	1.98	2.00	2.04	1.97	2.07	2.20	1.94	2.00	2.09	2.16	2.01	1.99	2.14	2.00	2.16
Standard deviation	0.89	0.89	0.89	0.82	0.82	0.90	0.88	0.91	0.98	0.82	0.92	0.88	0.93	0.92	0.88	0.92	0.83	0.87
Standard error	0.03	0.04	0.04	0.09	0.06	0.06	0.07	0.08	0.07	0.05	0.06	0.06	0.06	0.06	0.06	0.06	0.07	0.09

- As for variation in standards across the UK, two-thirds (65 percent) believe that a variation in quality is a price worth paying for local elected control of public services. This holds fast right across the social spectrum - and across different UK regions.
- The Local Voices poll suggests that British people want more local democratic input into their public services, including policing. They believe that variation in service is a price worth paying for locally elected authority over policing. In this context, the US model of local political control of police forces (with the greater local accountability that follows) appears to chime with what the British public wants.
- Local voices <u>want</u> local choices.

Q2: How accountable do you believe the people who run your local public services are to you for their decisions and performance?

	Total	Sex		Age						Social Class				Region				
		Male	Female	18-24	25-34	35-44	45-54	55-64	65+	AB	C1	C2	DE	South East	Mid-lands	North Eng-land	Wales & South West	Scot-land
Unweighted base	1000	470	530	90	183	208	181	135	203	302	267	206	225	270	246	252	142	90
Weighted base	1000	486	514	109	195	190	170	131	204	232	274	218	276	266	258	250	137	89
Net accountable	456 / 46%	196 / 40%	260 / 51%	65 / 60%	99 / 51%	82 / 43%	59 / 35%	55 / 42%	96 / 47%	101 / 44%	133 / 49%	92 / 42%	131 / 47%	126 / 48%	112 / 44%	116 / 46%	55 / 40%	46 / 52%
Very accountable (4)	114 / 11%	49 / 10%	65 / 13%	8 / 7%	24 / 13%	16 / 8%	20 / 12%	21 / 16%	24 / 12%	22 / 9%	33 / 12%	29 / 13%	31 / 11%	35 / 13%	27 / 10%	29 / 12%	13 / 9%	10 / 11%
Somewhat accountable (3)	342 / 34%	147 / 30%	195 / 38%	57 / 52%	75 / 38%	66 / 35%	39 / 23%	34 / 26%	71 / 35%	79 / 34%	101 / 37%	62 / 28%	100 / 36%	91 / 34%	86 / 33%	87 / 35%	42 / 31%	36 / 40%
Not very accountable (2)	341 / 34%	175 / 36%	166 / 32%	30 / 27%	65 / 33%	66 / 35%	73 / 43%	51 / 39%	56 / 27%	88 / 38%	90 / 33%	76 / 35%	88 / 32%	88 / 33%	93 / 36%	78 / 31%	50 / 36%	32 / 36%
Not at all accountable (1)	166 / 17%	99 / 20%	67 / 13%	9 / 9%	25 / 13%	39 / 21%	33 / 19%	19 / 15%	40 / 19%	37 / 16%	44 / 16%	40 / 18%	45 / 16%	41 / 15%	45 / 18%	47 / 19%	25 / 18%	8 / 9%
Net unaccountable	507 / 51%	275 / 57%	233 / 45%	39 / 36%	90 / 46%	106 / 56%	107 / 63%	70 / 53%	95 / 47%	124 / 54%	134 / 49%	116 / 53%	133 / 48%	129 / 48%	138 / 54%	125 / 50%	75 / 55%	40 / 45%
Don't know	36 / 4%	15 / 3%	21 / 4%	5 / 4%	6 / 3%	3 / 2%	5 / 3%	6 / 5%	12 / 6%	7 / 3%	7 / 2%	11 / 5%	12 / 5%	11 / 4%	7 / 3%	8 / 3%	7 / 5%	3 / 3%
Mean	2.42	2.31	2.52	2.61	2.52	2.31	2.28	2.46	2.42	2.38	2.46	2.39	2.44	2.47	2.37	2.41	2.33	2.56
Standard deviation	0.91	0.92	0.89	0.76	0.88	0.90	0.92	0.95	0.96	0.87	0.91	0.95	0.91	0.92	0.90	0.94	0.90	0.82
Standard error	0.03	0.04	0.04	0.08	0.07	0.06	0.07	0.08	0.07	0.05	0.06	0.07	0.06	0.06	0.06	0.06	0.08	0.09

Q3: Would you like to have more input into the priorities set for your loca public services and have the people who run them be more accountable to you or not?

	Total	Sex		Age						Social Class				Region				
		Male	Female	18-24	25-34	35-44	45-54	55-64	65+	AB	C1	C2	DE	South East	Mid-lands	North Eng-land	Wales & South West	Scot-land
Unweighted base	1000	470	530	90	183	208	181	135	203	302	267	206	225	270	246	252	142	90
Weighted base	1000	486	514	109	195	190	170	131	204	232	274	218	276	266	258	250	137	89
Yes	795 / 80%	395 / 81%	400 / 78%	78 / 71%	157 / 81%	159 / 84%	151 / 89%	102 / 78%	147 / 72%	193 / 83%	213 / 78%	174 / 80%	215 / 78%	211 / 79%	216 / 84%	193 / 77%	109 / 79%	66 / 74%
No	175 / 17%	81 / 17%	94 / 18%	28 / 26%	34 / 17%	25 / 13%	16 / 10%	25 / 19%	46 / 23%	35 / 15%	54 / 20%	41 / 19%	45 / 16%	43 / 16%	38 / 15%	51 / 20%	22 / 16%	20 / 23%
Don't know	30 / 3%	10 / 2%	20 / 4%	3 / 3%	4 / 2%	6 / 3%	3 / 2%	4 / 3%	10 / 5%	3 / 1%	7 / 3%	3 / 2%	17 / 6%	11 / 4%	4 / 2%	6 / 2%	6 / 4%	2 / 3%

Q4: If there were local elections in your area on 2nd May, would you be more likely to vote in the local election if you were also given an opportunity to elect the people who run your local public services – such as the local Chief Constable of Police or the Chief Executive of the local NHS trust?

	Total	Sex		Age						Social Class				Region				
		Male	Fe-male	18-24	25-34	35-44	45-54	55-64	65+	AB	CI	C2	DE	South East	Mid-lands	North Eng-land	Wales & South West	Scot-land
Unweighted base	1000	470	530	90	183	208	181	135	203	302	267	206	225	270	246	252	142	90
Weighted base	1000	486	514	109	195	190	170	131	204	232	274	218	276	266	258	250	137	89
Net likely	479 48%	239 49%	240 47%	55 50%	125 64%	97 51%	76 45%	53 40%	72 35%	105 45%	141 52%	109 50%	124 45%	126 47%	130 50%	112 45%	67 49%	43 48%
A lot more likely	285 29%	147 30%	138 27%	22 20%	71 36%	72 38%	45 26%	32 25%	43 21%	62 27%	88 32%	62 28%	74 27%	73 27%	74 29%	76 30%	34 25%	29 32%
A bit more likely	193 19%	92 19%	102 20%	33 30%	54 28%	25 13%	32 19%	21 16%	29 14%	43 19%	54 20%	47 21%	50 18%	54 20%	56 22%	36 14%	33 24%	14 16%
Not much more likely	51 5%	26 5%	25 5%	5 5%	4 2%	14 7%	10 6%	5 4%	12 6%	9 4%	14 5%	11 5%	17 6%	22 8%	14 5%	9 4%	2 1%	4 5%
Would it make no difference to your likelihood of voting	436 44%	211 43%	225 44%	49 45%	59 30%	76 40%	80 47%	70 53%	103 51%	111 48%	110 40%	93 42%	123 44%	105 39%	106 41%	119 48%	66 48%	39 44%
Net unlikely	487 49%	236 49%	250 49%	54 49%	63 32%	90 47%	90 53%	75 57%	115 56%	119 52%	124 45%	104 47%	139 50%	127 48%	120 46%	128 51%	68 50%	43 49%
Don't know	35 3%	11 2%	24 5%	1 1%	7 3%	3 2%	4 2%	4 3%	17 8%	8 3%	8 3%	6 3%	13 5%	13 5%	8 3%	10 4%	2 1%	3 3%

Q5: Do you think the standards of local public services would improve, stay about the same or get worse if local people elected the people who run them?

	Total	Sex		Age						Social Class				Region				
		Male	Fe-male	18-24	25-34	35-44	45-54	55-64	65+	AB	CI	C2	DE	South East	Mid-lands	North Eng-land	Wales & South West	Scot-land
Unweighted base	1000	470	530	90	183	208	181	135	203	302	267	206	225	270	246	252	142	90
Weighted base	1000	486	514	109	195	190	170	131	204	232	274	218	276	266	258	250	137	89
Improve	585 58%	287 59%	298 58%	68 62%	116 59%	124 65%	100 58%	86 66%	91 45%	136 59%	164 60%	135 62%	149 54%	156 59%	148 57%	152 61%	77 56%	52 59%
Stay the same	264 26%	123 25%	142 28%	30 28%	56 28%	41 22%	45 26%	30 23%	62 31%	65 28%	68 25%	57 26%	75 27%	70 26%	67 26%	59 24%	41 30%	27 30%
Get Worse	72 7%	46 9%	26 5%	7 7%	11 6%	11 6%	15 9%	9 7%	19 9%	13 6%	25 9%	12 6%	22 8%	16 6%	21 8%	18 7%	11 8%	6 7%
Don't know	79 8%	30 6%	48 9%	4 3%	12 6%	14 7%	11 7%	6 4%	31 15%	17 8%	17 6%	14 6%	30 11%	24 9%	22 9%	20 8%	8 6%	4 4%

Q6: If local people elected the people who run their local public services, it is likely that the elected managers would try different approaches in different parts of the country and that some of them would suceed in improving standards of the services they run and that others would not. Do you think that a variation in the standard of public services in different areas of the country would be a price worth paying?

	Total	Sex		Age						Social Class				Region				
		Male	Fe-male	18-24	25-34	35-44	45-54	55-64	65+	AB	CI	C2	DE	South East	Mid-lands	North Eng-land	Wales & South West	Scot-land
Unweighted base	1000	470	530	90	183	208	181	135	203	302	267	206	225	270	246	252	142	90
Weighted base	1000	486	514	109	195	190	170	131	204	232	274	218	276	266	258	250	137	89
Yes	649 65%	334 69%	316 61%	76 69%	132 67%	122 64%	113 67%	75 57%	132 65%	160 69%	177 65%	144 66%	169 61%	165 62%	172 67%	158 63%	89 65%	65 73%
No	217 22%	105 22%	111 22%	21 19%	48 25%	41 22%	33 19%	36 27%	37 18%	54 23%	64 23%	49 22%	49 18%	56 21%	59 23%	58 23%	29 21%	14 16%
Don't know	134 13%	47 10%	87 17%	12 11%	16 8%	27 14%	24 14%	20 15%	35 17%	18 8%	33 12%	26 12%	58 21%	45 17%	27 10%	34 14%	19 14%	10 11%

Appendix B: Police Force performance league tables

Extracts from *How Is Your Police Force Performing? A Comprehensive Analysis of Police Performance Data*, a report written and compiled by Charles Banner, Nicholas Boles and Anna Reid, which was published by Policy Exchange in September 2002. A full copy of the report can be downloaded from: http://www.policyexchange.org.uk/record.jsp?type=research&ID=6

Detailed commentary on methodology

1. The Model: Domains and Spidergrams

Policy Exchange's performance league tables for police forces in England and Wales use performance data derived from the Home Office, Her Majesty's Inspectorate of Constabulary, the Crown Prosecution Service and the British Crime Survey for end-April 2000 to end-April 2002.

This is the first assessment of police performance to follow the new 'Domains' format proposed by the Home Office for its own 'Policing Performance Assessment Framework', due for launch in April 2004.

Accordingly, we have grouped police force performance indicators into four categories or 'Domains':
(i)   Crime Rates
(ii) Operational Effectiveness
(iii) Economic Efficiency
(iv) Public Reassurance
Other Domains currently being considered by the Home Office - 'Community-building', 'Working with Criminal Justice Agencies', 'Helping the Public' - we have left out as being hard to measure and less central to the policing function.

Performance in all four Domains is represented in a single chart bearing multiple axes - the 'spidergram' or 'performance radar' - in order that it can be seen to what extent a force's good performance in one category is achieved at the expense of other aspects of policing. Consistent performance across all Domains would be represented by a square shape on the spidergram; distortions such as kite shapes depict inconsistent levels of performance across the different categories.

Forces are also ranked in league tables, based on an overall performance score calculated from the four Domain Scores.

2. Performance Indicators within the Domains

We have excluded performance indicators (PIs) reckoned by the Home Office and HMIC to be unacceptably inconsistent and/or loosely defined - for example, forces' own user satisfaction surveys, and numbers of public order incidents. Controversial PIs such as percentage success rates on target times for responding to 999 calls have also been omitted.

The PIs making up each Domain are as follows:

Domain 1: Crime Rates
- Crimes per 1000 population.
- % Change in crimes per 1000 population on previous year.
- % Victims of burglary who have already been burgled in the past twelve months.
- % Victims of domestic violence who have already suffered domestic violence in the past twelve months.
  – The repeat burglary and repeat domestic crime

indicators are included because they provide a measure of how well forces are serving the most victimised members of the community, and most crime-rife parts of their force area. They were each given half weightings.

Domain 2: Operational Effectiveness
- % of recorded crime detected.
  - For this PI we included 'non-administrative' (also known as 'sanctioned') detections only. These are offences where a suspect has been charged, summonsed or cautioned, or asked for an offence to be taken into consideration by a court.
  - We excluded 'administrative' detections - offences where no further action is taken by the police because the victim refuses to give evidence because the offender or an essential witness is ill or dies, because the offender is under the age of criminal responsibility, because the six-month time limit for commencing proceedings has been exceeded, or because the police or CPS decide that proceedings would serve no useful purpose.
- % of people arrested who are later charged, summonsed or cautioned, or who ask for an offence to be taken into account by a court.
- % of cases presented to the CPS that are pursued to completion in court (i.e. where the prosecution was not dropped). This includes cases that the CPS initially sends back to the police with a request for more evidence, but which are eventually pursued to completion.

Domain 3: Economic Efficiency
- Net revenue expenditure per detection. This excludes capital spending and takes into account non-administrative detections only.
- Change in recorded crime numbers per £1m of net revenue expenditure.
- Average number of days' sick leave taken per officer.

Domain 4: Public Reassurance

- Number of complaints per 1000 officers.
  - This includes all complaints recorded under Section 69 of the Police Act 1996. They are against specified individuals or groups of individuals and usually relate to incivility, misconduct or allegations of criminality.
- The average of the percentages of respondents to the British Crime Survey declaring themselves 'very' worried about being burgled, 'very or fairly' worried about having their car stolen or broken into, or 'very or fairly' worried about mugging, rape, or racially motivated attack.
  - For details of this PI (Best Value PI #121) see p177 of the BCS bulletin *Crime in England and Wales 2001/02*, by John Simmons and colleagues, published by the Home Office in July 2002.
- % of respondents to the British Crime Survey who state that they consider there to be a high level of public disorder in their area. 'Public disorder' encompasses drunkenness and rowdiness, vandalism, drug dealing, minor racial abuse and teenagers hanging around.
  - For details of this PI (Best Value PI #122) see p177 of *Crime in England and Wales 2001/02*.
  - The 2001/02 British Crime Survey was compiled from 33,000 interviews undertaken in 2001 and 2002, but asked correspondents to recall incidents over the previous 12 months. The 12-month period to which the survey most closely correlates is the year to end-September 2001.

3. Calculations

Each force was given a 'Score' for each PI, representing its performance in relation to the nationwide average. Since most, if not all, PIs produced a fairly narrow range of results, with a clearly discernable 'baseline' that was achieved by even the worst performers, the Score was calculated by looking at the range rather than the actual numbers themselves. This was to ensure that good performance in a PI where the range was 18-30 would be rewarded the same as good performance in a PI where the range was 78-90. The equations used were as follows:

Where a high PI = best (eg. detection rates)

$$Z_i = \left[\frac{X_i - L}{Mean\,[Y_{i...xlii}] - L} \right] \times 100, -100$$

Where Xi-xlii are the data entries for each force, L and H are the lowest/highest entries, Z is the 'Score'.

Where a low PI = best (eg. crime rates)

$$Z_i = \left[\frac{H - X_i}{H - Mean\,[Y_{i...xlii}]} \right] \times 100, -100$$

Where Xi-xlii are the data entries for each force, L and H are the lowest/highest entries, Z is the 'Score'.

A score of 0 indicates that a force performs exactly averagely. A positive score indicates better-then-average performance; negative scores depict worse-than-average performance. To calculate overall Domain Scores for each force, we averaged PI scores in each Domain. In some cases, PIs were given half weightings. The Overall Scores for force performance were calculated by averaging the four Domain Scores, each having an equal weighting.

4. Grouping of comparable forces

We used two separate methods to gather forces into comparable groups. The first was to use the 'most similar forces' lists drawn up the Home Office in 1997. These were based on complex 'cluster analysis' of the following force area characteristics: % of unemployed who are men aged under 25; % of households living in rented accommodation; % one-parent families; percentage of the population living in very densely populated areas; % of the area that is very sparsely populated. They do not gather forces into distinct groups, but allot each force 3-9 other forces most similar to it. This means that although Force A may compare itself to Force B, Force B does not necessarily compare itself to Force A.

Our second, cruder but conceptually simpler, method was to map force areas along two axes, showing popula-tion density and % unemployment, and divide each axis along the mean. The four forces covering exceptionally densely populated conurbations - London, Birmingham, Manchester and Liverpool - were treated separately.

Five groups of very broadly comparable forces were created by this second method:

i)   Major Conurbations

ii)   Smaller Cities (relatively high population density, relatively high unemployment)

iii)   Rich Suburban (relatively high population density, relatively low unemployment)

iv)   Poor Rural (relatively low population density, relatively high unemployment)

v)   Rich Rural (relatively low population density, relatively low unemployment)

5. Caveats

Crime recording rules have become more rigorous in recent years, with the adoption of new recording standards in 1998 and again on April 1st 2002. Both these changes have resulted in a rise in recorded crime, though underlying crime rates, according to the British Crime Survey, have fallen over the period.

Consequently, forces that adopted April 2002's National Crime Recording Standard early appear to be performing worse than they actually are. Early adopters of the NCRS were Avon & Somerset, Cumbria, Lancashire, North Wales, Staffordshire and West Mercia. Partial early adopters were Kent, Northumbria and West Midlands.

Some types of crime are easier to solve than others, meaning that detection rates vary according to the crime pattern of any given area. Crime patterns are similar, however, in sociologically and demographically similar areas, meaning that the overall detection rate remains a useful measure of performance within groups of compa-rable forces.

The percentage of cases presented to the CPS that are pursued to completion in court is a measure of CPS efficiency as well as of the police's success in preparing cases and cooperating with prosecutors. A small number of cases are also abandoned by the CPS through no fault of the police, but on public interest grounds. Such cases include those where the court is likely to impose only a nominal penalty, where prosecution is likely to harm the victim's physical or mental health, where the defendant is elderly or suffering from mental or physical illness, where the defendant has put right the harm caused, or where details may be made public that risk harming international relations or national security.

It is worth noting that high numbers of complaints per officer (a performance indicator in our Public Satisfaction Domain) do not reflect entirely badly on a force, since they indicate faith on the part of the public that complaints are worth lodging, as well as dissatisfaction with performance. Low complaint numbers may indicate distrust of and alienation from the police, rather than satisfaction. We have nevertheless included complaints in our indicators, alongside 'fear of crime' and 'perceived public disorder' measures from the British Crime Survey.

6. Unobtainable data
We were unable to include the following data:

Domain 1: Crime Rates
In 2001/02 one force failed to report levels of repeat burglaries, and six failed to report levels of repeat domestic crime. For the purpose of overall Domain Score calculations, we assumed that they performed averagely in these areas. In 2000/01 one force failed to report levels of repeat burglaries, and eleven failed to report levels of repeat domestic crime.

Domain 2: Operational Effectiveness:
The Home Office will not be releasing arrest numbers for 2001/02 until October. The PI '% of arrestees who are later charged/summonsed/cautioned/have an offence taken into account in another criminal proceeding' was therefore omitted from the 2001/02 calculations. South Yorkshire did not report on this in 2000/01, and was assumed to have performed averagely.

In 2001/02 and 2000/01 Durham failed to report non-administrative detection rates. We assumed that it performed averagely in this area.

Domain 3: Economic Efficiency:
Durham's failure to report 2001/02 non-administrative detection rates also meant that we were unable to calculate spending per detection. We assumed that it performed averagely. Five forces have not yet reported net revenue expenditure for 2001/02, with the result that we were unable to calculate spending per detection or crimes reduced per £1m spend for these forces. We assumed that they performed averagely in these areas.

Domain 4: Public Reassurance:
The British Crime Survey was greatly expanded in 2001/02, with the result that this was the first year in which it produced data at force level rather than regional level. Thus force-by-force 'levels of anxiety about crime' and 'perceived levels of public disorder' PIs were therefore unavailable for our 2000/01 calculations. In order to prevent extreme 'Complaints' results from having undue influence on the 2000/01 Overall Score, universal average performance (0.00) was assumed in the two BCS-based PIs; the Domain Score was then calculated, as in 2001/02, from an average of all three PI Scores.

Findings and conclusions

1. Main findings
Police force performance varies widely, irrespective of force size or type of area covered. Even when grouped into 'most comparable forces', taking into account population density and socio-economic data such as male youth unemployment, % social housing etc, differences in performance are dramatic. Forces doing markedly better than the norm for the type of area they cover are Dyfed Powys, Gwent, Devon and Cornwall and Northumbria. Poor performers include Nottinghamshire, West Yorkshire and Sussex.

All the forces consistently heading the league table are traditional county-based ones. Large amalgamated forces such as Thames Valley perform no better than small, county-based ones such as Suffolk or Hampshire.

There is however a clear link between performance and population density. Of the top ten forces on overall performance in 2001/02, eight cover rural or semi-rural southern English or Welsh counties. Welsh forces scored particularly well, with Dyfed Powys heading the table both for 2000/01 and 2001/02. Dyfed's Chief Constable attributes this to his county's extremely low population and to the fact that he has the resources to investigate even very minor crimes, and to his policy of keeping small local police stations open. More remarkable is Gwent's excellent performance; whereas Dyfed covers the most thinly populated region of England and Wales, Gwent includes the small city of Newport and depressed former mining towns.

Five out of the seven metropolitan forces[7] appeared at or near the bottom of the table in both 2000/01 and 2001/02, although in the case of the West Midlands this was probably partly due to its early adoption of a new more rigorous crime recording standard.

Most forces performed similarly in 2000/01 and 2001/02, with a few exceptions. Cambridgeshire, Kent and Surrey improved their performance dramatically over the period. North Wales and West Mercia appeared to deteriorate in performance, although this was probably due to their early adoption of a new crime recording standard (see Methodology-Caveats for details).

The spidergrams demonstrate that nearly all of the nine forces[8] praised by the Government for having greatly reduced street crime in recent months performed relatively badly on most aspects of performance, not just the 'Crime Rates' Domain.

Conclusions

Given that large forces perform no better than small ones overall, and that the forces consistently heading the league table are all traditional county-based ones, the Home Office should be wary of further force amalgamations or of replacing current structures with regional 'superforces'.

In view of the wide variety in performance between forces covering comparable areas, more transparent mechanisms should be set up whereby forces can learn from each other's successes and failures, and senior officers can be held accountable for their forces' performance.

There is a case for allocating more revenue to forces covering the largest and most densely populated conurbations, notably Greater Manchester and the Metropolitan Police. Currently, the Office of the Deputy Prime Minister (now responsible for local government) uses a grant allocation formula based on population size and density, various socio-economic measures, number of motorway junctions and pension commitments. It can be argued that the formula does not take sufficient account of the higher number of crimes per head of population and greater difficulty in investigating crime that are experienced in the biggest cities; thus might be explained big-city forces' consistent appearance at the bottom of the league table. On the other hand, when this point has been raised in the past, smaller forces have objected that to increase grant to forces with rising crime rates, and reduce grant to forces with falling ones would be to reward failure and penalize success.

The bureaucratic effort involved in defining, collecting and ensuring the consistency across forces of Performance Indicators (PIs) is immense. Forces are currently required by the Home Office to track eighteen 'Best Value Performance Indicators', which subdivide into thirty plus actual datapoints. Many of these are of doubtful utility and some may in fact be counterproductive; for example, target times for 999 responses have been blamed for a rise in road deaths caused by speeding police cars. The Home Office and Inspectorate of Constabulary (HMIC) should keep the number of PIs to a minimum, be alert to the possibility of perverse incentives, and not devote more resources to PI collection and audit than they are worth.

Notes

7   The seven metropolitan forces are: Metropolitan, West Midlands, Merseyside, Greater Manchester, West Yorkshire, South Yorkshire and Northumbria.

8   Avon & Somerset, Greater Manchester, Metropolitan, Merseyside, Nottinghamshire, South Yorkshire, Thames Valley, West Midlands and West Yorkshire.

Policy Exchange police research: 2001/02 overall scores

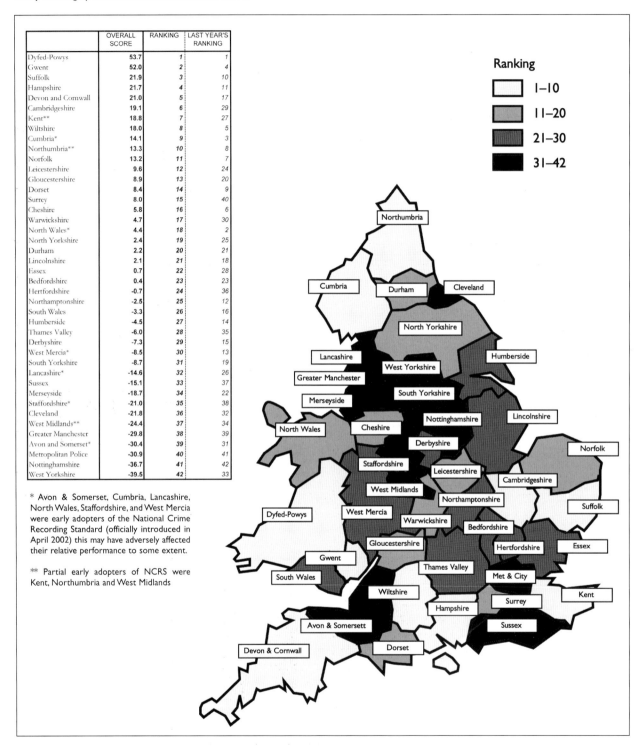

	OVERALL SCORE	RANKING	LAST YEAR'S RANKING
Dyfed-Powys	53.7	1	1
Gwent	52.0	2	4
Suffolk	21.9	3	10
Hampshire	21.7	4	11
Devon and Cornwall	21.0	5	17
Cambridgeshire	19.1	6	29
Kent**	18.8	7	27
Wiltshire	18.0	8	5
Cumbria*	14.1	9	3
Northumbria**	13.3	10	8
Norfolk	13.2	11	7
Leicestershire	9.6	12	24
Gloucestershire	8.9	13	20
Dorset	8.4	14	9
Surrey	8.0	15	40
Cheshire	5.8	16	6
Warwickshire	4.7	17	30
North Wales*	4.4	18	2
North Yorkshire	2.4	19	25
Durham	2.2	20	21
Lincolnshire	2.1	21	18
Essex	0.7	22	28
Bedfordshire	0.4	23	23
Hertfordshire	-0.7	24	36
Northamptonshire	-2.5	25	12
South Wales	-3.3	26	16
Humberside	-4.5	27	14
Thames Valley	-6.0	28	35
Derbyshire	-7.3	29	15
West Mercia*	-8.5	30	13
South Yorkshire	-8.7	31	19
Lancashire*	-14.6	32	26
Sussex	-15.1	33	37
Merseyside	-18.7	34	22
Staffordshire*	-21.0	35	38
Cleveland	-21.8	36	32
West Midlands**	-24.4	37	34
Greater Manchester	-29.8	38	39
Avon and Somerset*	-30.4	39	31
Metropolitan Police	-30.9	40	41
Nottinghamshire	-36.7	41	42
West Yorkshire	-39.5	42	33

* Avon & Somerset, Cumbria, Lancashire, North Wales, Staffordshire, and West Mercia were early adopters of the National Crime Recording Standard (officially introduced in April 2002) this may have adversely affected their relative performance to some extent.

** Partial early adopters of NCRS were Kent, Northumbria and West Midlands

Ranking

- 1–10
- 11–20
- 21–30
- 31–42

Force Performance Comparisons: Policy Exchange Force Families

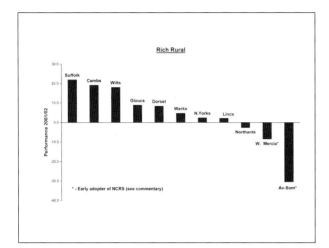

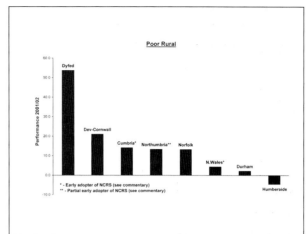

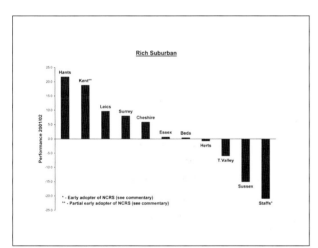

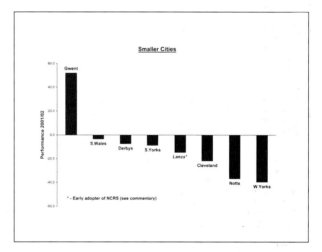

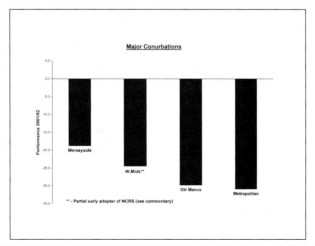

Sample 'Spidergrams' or 'Performance Radars'

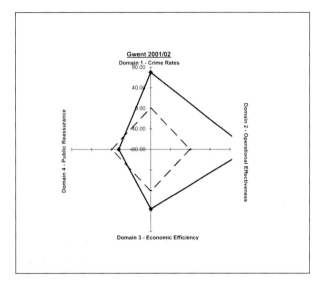

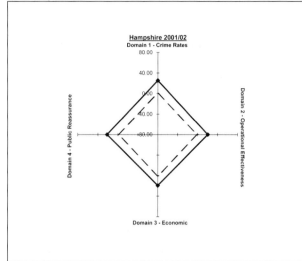

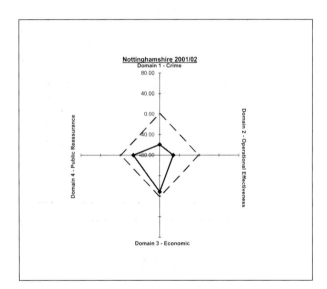

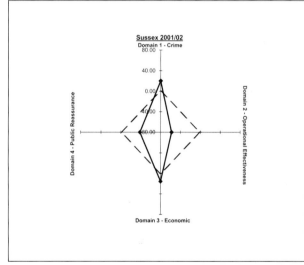

These examples demonstrate the value of the 'spidergrams' in depicting a police force's performance in the round. For instance, the publication of crime rates alone would suggest that Sussex Police Force's performance in 2000/01 was considerably above average (represented by the dotted-line square), whereas the spidergram above indicates that its overall performance was less impressive.

Hampshire, in contrast, does slightly better than average on all counts. This is particularly pertinent when considering such initiatives as the 'safer streets' campaign, which focus on a single issue at the expense of other important police responsibilities.

Force Performance Comparisons: Home Office Force Families

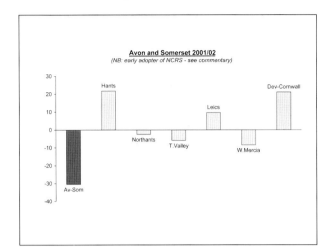

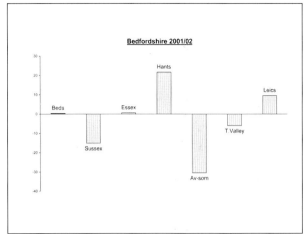

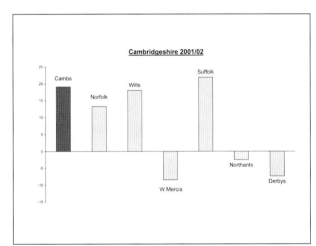

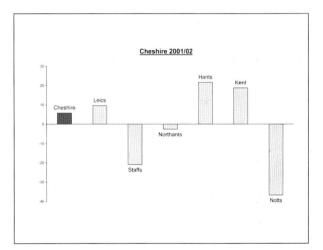

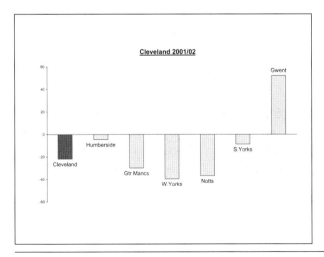

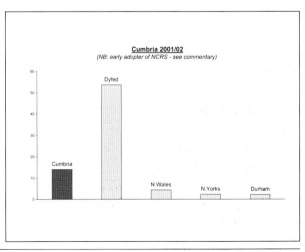

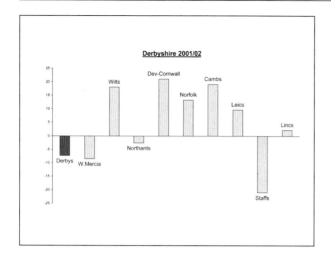

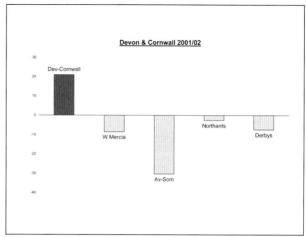

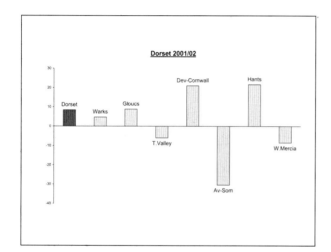

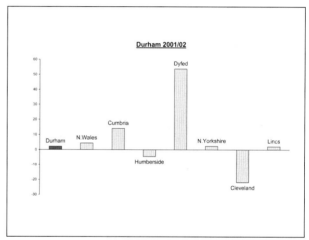

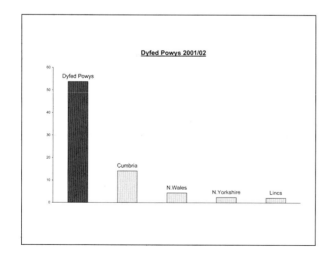

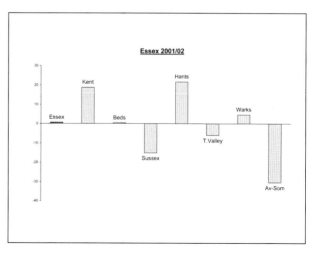

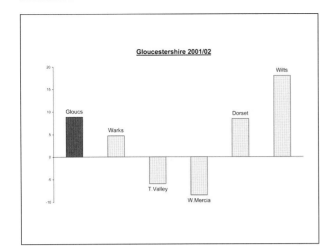

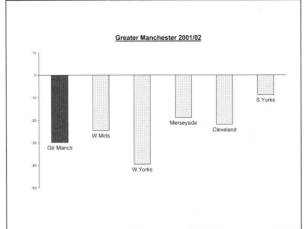

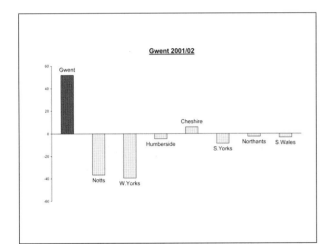

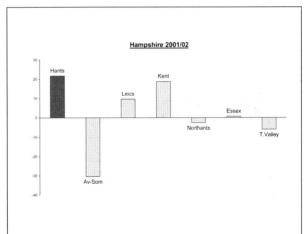

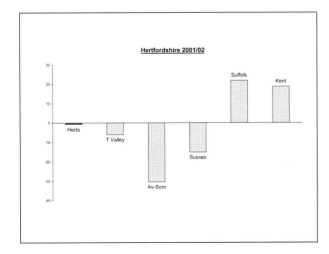

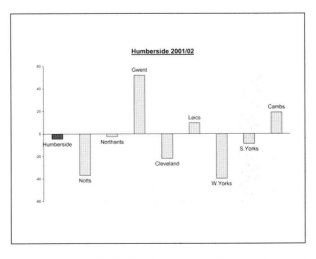

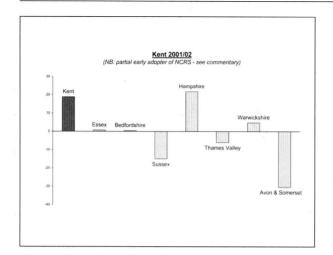

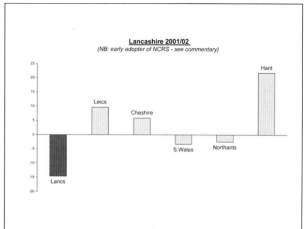

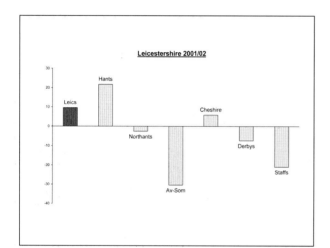

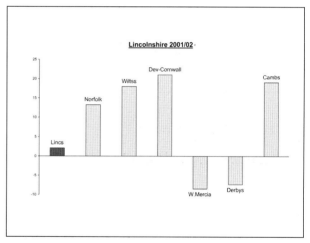

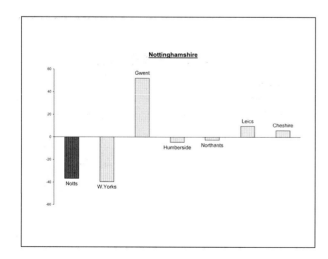

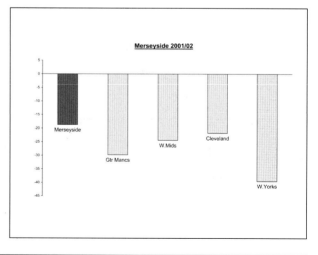

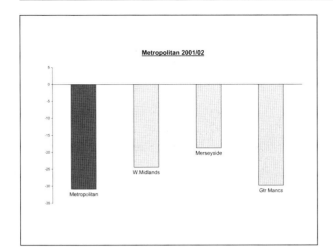

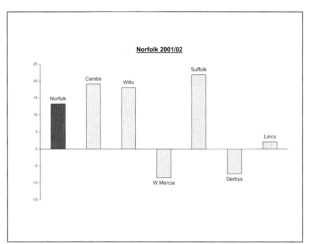

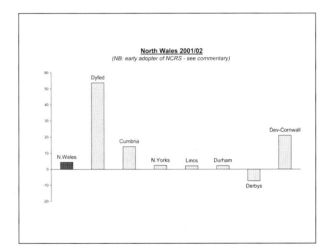

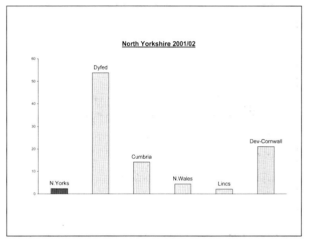

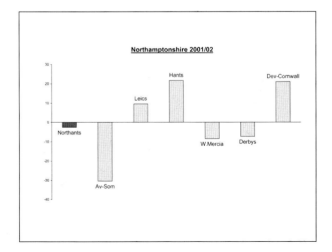

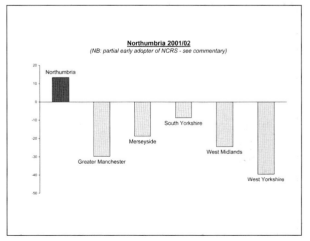

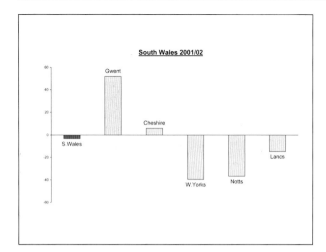

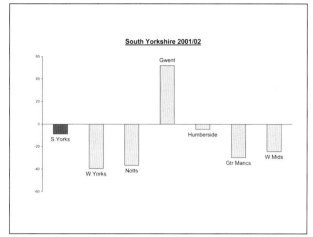

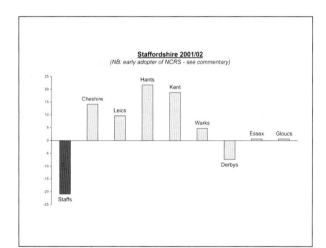

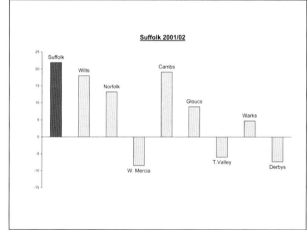

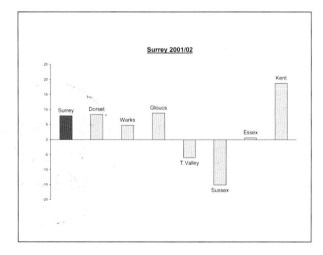

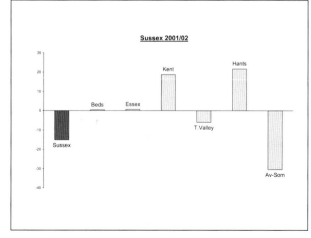

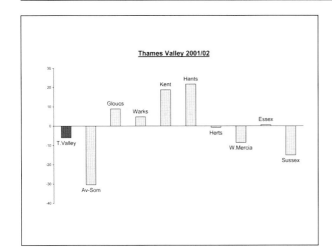

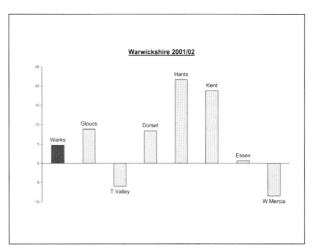

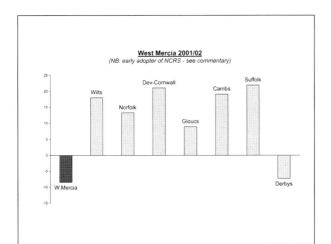

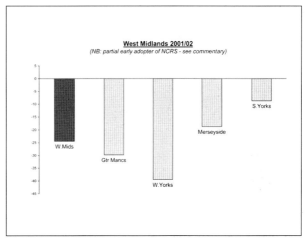

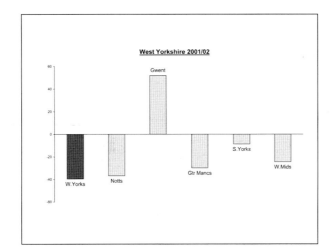

Bibliography

England and Wales: Legislation, parliamentary debates and inspection reports
Crime and Disorder Act 1998, HMSO 1998
Police Reform Act 2002, Chapter 30, HMSO 2002
Explanatory notes, Police Reform Act 2002, Chapter 30, HMSO 2002
Modernising Government, White Paper, HMSO 1999
A New Beginning: Policing in Northern Ireland. The report of the Independent Commission on
    policing for Northern Ireland, HMSO 1999
Policing a New Century: A Blueprint for Reform, White Paper, Command 5326, 2001
House of Commons Parliamentary Debates, Hansard Vol 388, No 174/5
House of Commons Home Affairs Committee, Police Reform Bill, Second report of session,
    2001-02 HC 612
House of Lords Parliamentary Debates, Hansard Vol 633/634/638
HMIC Thematic Report, *Police Integrity: Securing and Maintaining Public Confidence*, 1999.
HMIC Inspection Report, Dyfed Powys Constabulary 2001/02
HMIC Inspection Report, Kent County Constabulary 2001/2002
HMIC Primary Inspection Report, Kent County Constabulary 1997/98
HMIC Preliminary Inspection Report, on forces involved in the street crime initiative, May 2002
HMSO: Report into Police Rewards and Responsibilities, Sheehy 1993

England and Wales: books, papers and articles
Kent: The Next Four Years, Kent County Council 2002
A. Alexander 'Thinking Aloud about City Government', *Local Government Studies* Nov./Dec. 1986
L. Bridges 'Convictions without principle', *Criminal Justice Matters* No. 46, Winter 2001
E. Elliot Major 'A stick in carrot's clothing', *The Guardian* 9/4/1999
M. Fitzgerald, M. Hough, I. Joseph and T. Quereshi *Policing for London*, Willan 2002
B. Loveday 'The Impact of performance Culture on Criminal Justice Agencies in England and
    Wales' *International Journal of the Sociology of Law* Vol. 27, 1998
B. Loveday 'Improving the Status of Police Patrol' *International Journal of the Sociology of Law*
    Vol. 26, 1998
B. Loveday 'Joint Boards and the Local Accountability of Police in the Metropolitan Areas',
    Local Government Studies, March/April 1990
L. Lustgarten *The Governance of the Police*, Sweet and Maxwell 1986
C. Marchant 'Facts and Figures', *Police Review* 18/10/02
G. Marshall in *Police and Government* Methuen 1965
M.K. Nalla 'Perspectives on the Growth of Police Bureaucracies, 1948-1984: an Examination of
    the Explanations' *Policing and Society* No. 3, 1992
P. Neyroud and A. Beckley *Policing, Ethics and Human Rights*, Willan 2001
M. O'Byrne *Changing Policing: Revolution not Evolution*, Russell House Publishing 2001
T. Orr Munro 'Police Standards Unit intervenes to help forces meet crime targets' *Police
    Review* 27/9/02
'Chief constables back plans to tackle street crime in robbery hotspots' *Police Review* 22/3/02
PA Consulting *Diary of a Police Officer*, Police Research Series paper 149, Home Office 2001
R. Reiner *The Politics of the Police*, OUP 2000
A. Rutherford *Criminal Justice Choices: What is Criminal Justice For?*, IPPR 2000
S. Savage, S. Charman and S. Cope *Policing and The Power of Persuasion*, Blackstone 2000
C. Sparks and S. Spencer *Them and Us? The Public, Offenders and the Criminal Justice System*,
    IPPR 2002

USA
J. Butts and J. Travis *The Rise and Fall of American Youth Violence, 1980-2000*, Urban Institute, 2002
R. Giuliani *Leadership*, Little Brown 2002
R. Guiliani and H. Safir *Compstat: Leadership In Action*, NYPD, 1997
J. Maple *The Crime Fighter: How You Can Make your Community Crime-Free*, Broadway Books, 1999
E.R. Moffit 'Rethinking the Role of the Police: Restructuring and the District of Columbia'
    Statement to Senate Subcommittee on Oversight, Evidence from The Heritage Foundation
    30/4/97
E.H. Monkennen *Police in Urban America*, CUP 1981
Muhlhausen D, 'Research Challenges Claim of COPS Effectiveness', The Heritage Foundation,
    Occasional Paper 4/4/02
G. Segal, A Moore and J Nolan 'California's Competitive Cities: A Report Card on Efficiency...'
    Reason Public Policy Institute, Policy Study no. 291, February 2002
E. B. Silverman *NYPD Battles Crime: Innovative Strategies in Policing*, Northeastern University
    Press, 1999
E.B. Silverman 'Mapping Change', *Law Enforcement News*, 1996
Transparency International *Corruption at the Local Government Level: the US Experience*, T.I.
    March 2002
G. Woods *The Police in Los Angeles*, Garland Publishing 1993

Netherlands
T. Jones *Policing and Democracy in the Netherlands*, PSI 1995
E.R. Muller 'Policing and Accountability in the Netherlands: A Happy Marriage or a Stressful
    Relationship?' forthcoming in *Policing and Society* 2003.
A. Osborn 'Party is over as Fortuyn's heirs feud' *The Observer* 20/10/02
'Fortuynism without Fortuyn', *The Economist* 30/11/02

France
C. Emsley *Policing in Europe*, Open University 1987
H. Horton *Policing Policy in France*, Policy Studies Institute, 1995
Interpol *International Crime Statistics*, 1999
C. Journes 'The Structure of the French Police System', *International Journal of the Sociology of
    Law*, Vol. 2, 1993
R. Levy *Police and Public in Paris: Prepared for New Visions of the European City*, NYU 2002
B. Loveday, 'Government and Accountability of the Police' in ed. E. Mawby *Policing Across the
    World: Issues for the 21st Century*, UCL Press 1999

On-the-record interviewees

UK
T. Godwin, Acting Deputy Assistant Commissioner, Territorial Policing HQ, Met
T. Grange, Chief Constable Dyfed Powys Constabulary
P. Kernaghan, Chief Constable Hampshire Constabulary
K. Flannery, Assistant Inspector (non-police), HMIC, Home Office
Councillor J. Chitty, Medway City Council
Councillor N. Dean, Sevenoaks District Council
M. Fallon MP Sevenoaks, Kent
Councillor A. Prodger, Medway City Council

USA
National Institute of Justice representatives T.E. Feucht, Deputy Director, B. Vila and R.
    Kaminski.
E. Lehrer, American Enterprise Institute, Washington DC
R.E. Moffet, Heritage Foundation, Washington DC
J. Travis, Urban Institute, Washington DC
K. Costello, Office of Chief of Police, NYPD
Lieutenant F. Dywer, Office of Chief of Operations   NYPD
Chief J. Esposito, Chief of Operations, NYPD
Captain H. Knoor, Office of Chief of Operations, NYPD
Public Information Officers M. Martin and J.T. Ritter, Police Department Arlington County,
    Virginia
Deputy Commissioner Operations J. McEntee, Baltimore Police Department
G. Wasserman, Senior Policy Adviser Philadelphia Police Department

Netherlands
Dr M.J. Bezuyen, Policy adviser to Mayor, City Hall, Amsterdam
Prof. E.R. Muller, Crisis Onderzoek Team (COT), The Hague
Senator U. Rosenthal, COT, The Hague
J. van der Steen, Deputy Director, Politie, The Hague
Dr. M. de la Torre, COT, The Hague

France
R. Levy, Centre Nationale de la Recherche Scientifique, Paris

Glossary

ACPO Association of Chief Police Officers
APA Association of Police Authorities
BVPI Best Value Performance Indicator
BCS British Crime Survey
BCU Basic Command Unit
CDRPs Crime and Disorder Reduction
Partnerships
COPS Community Orientated Policing Scheme
CPS Crown Prosecution Service
CSO Community Support Officer
FTE Full-time equivalent
GN Gendarmerie Nationale
HMIC Her Majesty's Inspectorate of
Constabulary
KLPD (Dutch) National Police Agency
KPM Kent Policing Model
LPF List Pym Fortuyn
NCRS National Crime Recording Standard
NIM National Intelligence Model
PD Police Department
PI Performance Indicator
PN Police Nationale
PSU Police Standards Unit
SCAG Street Crime Action Group